SO NOW YOU'RE THE
Superintendent!

SO NOW YOU'RE THE Superintendent!

John Eller ◆ Howard C. Carlson

A Joint Publication

CORWIN PRESS
A SAGE Company

AMERICAN ASSOCIATION
OF SCHOOL ADMINISTRATORS

For information:

Corwin Press
A SAGE Company
2455 Teller Road
Thousand Oaks, California 91320
www.corwinpress.com

SAGE Ltd.
1 Oliver's Yard
55 City Road
London, EC1Y 1SP
United Kingdom

SAGE Publications India Pvt. Ltd.
B 1/I 1 Mohan Cooperative
   Industrial Area
Mathura Road, New Delhi 110 044
India

SAGE Publications Asia-Pacific
   Pte. Ltd.
33 Pekin Street #02-01
Far East Square
Singapore 048763

Printed in the United States of America

Library of Congress Cataloging-in-Publication Data

Eller, John, 1957—
   So now you're the superintendent! / John Eller, Howard C. Carlson.
      p. cm.
   Includes bibliographical references and index.
   ISBN 978-1-4129-4171-6 (cloth)—ISBN 978-1-4129-4172-3 (pbk.)
   1. School superintendents—Training of—United States. 2. School management and organization—United States. I. Carlson, Howard C. II. Title.

LB1715.E495 2009
371.2'011–dc22

2008031916

This book is printed on acid-free paper.

14 10 9 8 7 6 5 4 3

Acquisitions Editor: Hudson Perigo
Editorial Assistant: Lesley K. Blake
Production Editor: Appingo Publishing Services
Cover Designer: Scott Van Atta
Graphic Designer: Brian Bello

Contents

Preface

Welcome to the Superintendency! The process and fanfare are over; you've been offered and accepted the job of superintendent. You know the complexities and responsibilities this job brings and you understand the amount of time and commitment that is required. You know that you will face difficult challenges, experience professional growth beyond your imagination, and enjoy many rewards as you make a positive difference in this institution that is so crucial to the community it serves.

But . . . what you do today, tomorrow, and next week to establish yourself as the instructional leader? How you find out what the staff and community expectations are for your performance? Where are the landmines that could be waiting for you around the corner? How do you build key relationships that will help you be successful and help the school district to keep moving forward? What kinds of techniques and strategies can you use to communicate to your stakeholders? How do you implement new ideas for honoring the accomplishments of the past?

THE DESIGN OF THIS BOOK

This book was designed as a practical guide to help you address these and many other situations and opportunities you will face as a superintendent, either new to the profession or new to the district. It was not designed to be a scholarly publication or a research book, even though many of the techniques and ideas contained inside are based on research. We know there are other books on the market that can provide you with theory and research about the school superintendency. This book fills a niche that exists in the application of theory in leadership and in the superintendency. The information contained in this book has been gathered from a variety of sources. We've used our experience as school superintendents, central office administrators, school principals, university professors, and leadership coaches to select the content for this book. We've also used information we have gathered from actual school superintendents we've worked with over the years.

WHO IS THIS BOOK DESIGNED FOR?

This book was primarily designed to assist leaders who are new to the superintendency; however, an interesting situation arose during the peer review process of our initial manuscript. Many of the reviewers were veteran school superintendents and they mentioned to us that there were ideas and strategies in the manuscript they found to be helpful reminders for them as they thought about getting ready for the upcoming year or were assuming new positions. Several reviewers also said the book would be a good source of information for those superintendents with some experience who are new to a district. In light of this feedback the book provides strategies and concepts that both superintendents and aspiring superintendents will find helpful.

LIMITATIONS OF THIS BOOK

Even with the comprehensive information provided, this book is somewhat limited in its approach. Leadership can be a complicated and district-specific endeavor. Some of the strategies outlined may not work in your particular situation or may need to be adjusted or modified to fit your specific situation. Because we have chosen to discuss a wide range of topics, we may not have addressed some of the topics in great depth. If you have particular needs that go beyond what we have provided related to a certain leadership behavior, you may need to consult other sources for assistance. We have tried to cover the major bases in relation to your needs for the first few years of your superintendency, but we know that it is impossible to provide every single resource new superintendents may need to be successful. Please keep the following in mind as you use this book:

- Even though the strategies and ideas outlined here have worked for others, they may need modification to work in your setting.
- Some of the strategies and ideas in this book fit better for some leadership styles than others. Carefully assess your own leadership style and see how you think it would fit within your selected strategy.
- The idea or strategy you are considering may be something entirely different than what your school district and its stakeholders have experienced in the past. In order to prepare them for this new way of thinking you may need to gradually get them ready for the new behavior. It may be necessary to "stage" or implement the strategy slowly.

- Gauge your own comfort level when selecting a possible idea or strategy. If you're not comfortable, it will be hard for you to follow through sincerely with the new idea.
- Develop an assessment plan so you can measure stakeholder response to the idea or strategy. This will let you know people's reactions and the proper pace for your implementation.

HOW TO USE THIS BOOK

The ten chapters in this book have been developed to address the most common issues faced by new superintendents. Even though they follow a sequence, the book has not been designed to be read from cover to cover. First focus on the areas that particularly interest you or meet a concern you have at the moment; read these sections first to help you address your needs. Once you have completed this first review of the material, branch out and look at the other information contained in the text. You will find interesting and informative information that will assist you as you encounter opportunities and challenges in your new role.

NEXT STEPS

We wish you well as you move forward into one of the most satisfying and challenging positions of your professional career. Your leadership has the potential to change lives and transform communities. Good luck on your journey and make the best of the experience!

Acknowledgments

Corwin Press gratefully acknowledges the contributions of the following reviewers:

Belinda G. Gimbert, PhD
Assistant Professor
The Ohio State University
School of Educational Policy
    and Leadership
College of Education and
    Human Ecology
Columbus, OH

Dr. Marian K. Hermie
Clinical Associate Professor
Arizona State University
Tempe, AZ

Janice Jackson
Lecturer and Senior Associate
    for the Executive Leadership
    Program for Education
Harvard Graduate School
    of Education
Cambridge, MA

James Jurs
Clinical Associate Professor
Mary Lou Fulton College of
    Education
Arizona State University
Tempe, AZ

John A. Roach, EdD
District Superintendent
Carlsbad Unified School District
Carlsbad, CA

Judith A. Rogers, EdD
Professional Learning Specialist
Tucson Unified School District
Tucson, AZ

About the Authors

John Eller is an assistant professor at Virginia Tech University teaching in the Educational Leadership Program in the National Capital Region. He teaches courses in the master's level Principal Preparation Program and the doctoral level programs in Educational Leadership. Dr. Eller is engaged in research in leadership, group dynamics, facilitation skills, and collaboration. He has been a school principal, the director of a training center, an assistant superintendent, and a university professor. In 1991 a school where he was principal was honored with a state award for curriculum innovation, and in 1994 he was named as the Iowa Principal of the Year and a National Distinguished Principal with the U.S. Department of Education.

John has his BS from Iowa State University, his MS from the University of Nebraska–Omaha, and his PhD from Loyola University–Chicago with an emphasis in leadership and organizational development.

John has worked with numerous schools, school districts, and other organizations over the years with a variety of content areas. He has consulted in emotional leadership skills, employee selection, recruitment and induction processes, effective management techniques, employee evaluation and supervision techniques, team building, dealing with difficult people, building interdependent work groups, effective communication skills, employee coaching skills, action research processes, effective instructional and presentation techniques, and a variety of other content areas. He has written numerous books over the years including *The Principals' Guide to Custodial Supervision, The Personal Planner and Training Guide for the Substitute Teacher, The Training Video Series for the Professional School Bus Driver* and Corwin Press titles *Energizing Staff Meetings* and *Effective Group Facilitation in Education: How to Energize Meetings and Manage Difficult Groups.*

 **Howard C. Carlson** is assistant superintendent for educational services in the Sunnyside Unified School District located in Tucson, Arizona. Carlson has previously served at the assistant superintendent and superintendent levels in the states of Washington and Minnesota. He has worked as president and CEO of a company which started schools in the states of Minnesota and Colorado and has consulted with school districts and private sector companies on a variety of educational issues. In addition to his current full-time position, he serves as a part-time faculty member at Walden University, where he works with students who are pursuing their doctorates in administrator leadership for teaching and learning. In 1990, he was recognized as the Washington State Young Agriculture Teacher of the Year and later as the Western Region of the United States Young Agriculture Teacher of the Year. In 1994 he was awarded the Washington Association of Agriculture Teachers' Association, District #4, Administrator of the Year, and in 2002 he was selected as a candidate for the Outstanding Young Minnesotan Award. In 2004 he was chosen, along with a select group of Minnesota superintendents, to meet with the Commissioner of the U.S. Department of Education to discuss the strengths and weaknesses of the No Child Left Behind (NCLB) law.

Carlson received his BS and doctorate from Washington State University and his master's degree from Heritage University. His doctoral study major was educational leadership and his minor was curriculum and instruction.

1

My Office Key Works, What's Next?

Do not go where the path may lead, go instead where there is no path and leave a trail.
—Ralph Waldo Emerson

Congratulations! You have just accepted a position that holds unlimited possibilities; the highs will likely mark the apex of your career, and the challenges will test you to the core. Does this sound interesting or unsettling? Is this the type of opportunity you were born to pursue, or a challenge that causes trepidation and fear? Welcome to the superintendency!

This brief description is consistent with the thoughts, feelings, and experiences you will face as you lead a school system. Marked by ever-increasing challenges, the superintendency is as tough a position as you will ever face in your career. Yet it provides an unmatched opportunity for changing children's lives forever. As the district's chief administrator, you will be faced with decisions that impact all students in your school system. As a teacher you likely had a greater impact on one individual, but as superintendent your work will touch each child's life. Sound exciting? It is!

ABOUT THIS CHAPTER

In this chapter we will discuss the position of superintendent—its context, background and history, and some of the complexities that come with the job. We will also include tips and strategies for surviving and thriving as you get started in the position and discuss various real life scenarios. From our own experiences and from our extensive discussions with practicing and former superintendents, we know that the position is very complex and community specific in nature. The ideas in this chapter and in this book were designed to address many of the situations you may face, but you will also need to use your own common sense and knowledge of the community to pave your path to success. As you study the ideas and strategies presented throughout this book do the following:

- Read the concepts presented; look for their core attributes or foundational theories. These are what you need to take away for your own implementation.
- Think about how the ideas and strategies fit your personality and comfort level; consider employing those that make the most sense to you.
- Examine the priorities and needs of the district you are serving; you may choose to use some ideas highlighted here before others because of their potential positive impact on your superintendency and the district.
- Talk with colleagues and mentors to find out their thoughts regarding the implementation of the ideas and strategies discussed throughout this book.
- Above all, use your own good common sense and intuition as you move forward!

Chapter 1 is designed to provide you with background and contextual information about the superintendency. This is important because once you understand the nature of the position, you can figure out how to transfer previous achievements to your new role, as well as make adaptations from former practices to be a successful superintendent. As we talk about the history and nature of the superintendency, we will sprinkle in ideas and strategies you may consider using. Some of these will be fully discussed in this chapter, while others will be introduced but explained in more detail elsewhere in the book. As you read this chapter, keep the following in mind:

- The historical background, the context, and the changing role of the position of superintendent in the United States and how these components relate to you and your priorities as the superintendent of your school district

- Ideas and strategies that you can use to successfully launch your superintendency
- Challenges of leading a school district and keeping the "Big Picture" in mind
- The Windowpane Model, which can help you analyze constituent perspectives
- The community liaison role of a superintendent and how this role relates to your behavior as the superintendent

THE SUPERINTENDENCY: UNDERSTANDING THE HISTORICAL CONTEXT

The job of a superintendent has been at the center of change and transition in American education for years. The American Association of School Administrators (AASA) completes a comprehensive study of the position every ten years. The data for this study is gathered using surveys of superintendents in the field. The latest study results are contained in their 2000 publication, *The Study of the American Superintendency,* (Glass, Björk, & Brunner, 2000). This comprehensive report outlines many interesting and important aspects of the position. It will provide you with good information about the experiences and perceptions of your colleagues in the field, plus help you understand the context of the position you have taken. You can obtain a copy of the report by contacting AASA at http:// www.aasa.org.

As you step into this highly rewarding but challenging position, it is important for you to understand the context of the job. We start this chapter with a brief overview of the historical background of the position of superintendent. The major researchers compiling the report (Glass, Björk, & Brunner, 2000) have developed an introductory section that does a great job outlining the history of the superintendency in the United States. Below is a summary of that history:

- In the early to mid-1800s, larger school systems in the United States employed a person as head of the schools called a superintendent.
- Over the years, the position became more formalized. New or aspiring superintendents were taught leadership skills in university preparation programs by the first school superintendents. These "pioneers" used knowledge they gained as practitioners to teach others how to do the job.
- The superintendency became associated with corporate models; lines of authority and roles between the board and superintendent became more formalized.

- Superintendents were seen as "experts" in the field of education, but sometimes their views conflicted with the feelings and wishes of the local community they served.
- Superintendent and board conflicts became more apparent in the 1990s, in some cases even involving power struggles.
- The present day superintendency is an increasingly complex venture because of state academic standards, budgetary issues, personnel concerns, and special interest group pressures. (Glass, Björk, & Brunner, 2000)

As you can see from this brief overview, the position of superintendent has been at the center of attention for a number of years. Many times the position has had some level of controversy associated with it. This is important for you to understand because if you are looking for a position where you can "melt into the woodwork," this will not be the right job for you. During your first thirty days on the job, keep this thought in mind: everyone in the community will know who you are or know of you. In essence, your job is somewhat like the president of the United States or some other public official; the things you say and do will be picked up and consumed by your community—so be careful! If you happen to be at a community event or the county fair, what you say or do will travel quickly through the community.

See how this principle plays out in the story of Walter:

Walter, the superintendent of a middle-sized school district, was seen as very friendly and outgoing, but at times would make statements that were thought to lack foresight. He knew from previous experience that he needed to be cognizant of what he said publicly, but sometimes the moment would get the best of him. An example from the previous summer played out when Walter participated in the community's Chamber of Commerce golf tournament. Walter was playing on a team that included business owners from the community. During a pause in their play, Walter observed that trees were being cut down near the golf course in preparation for a new manufacturing plant that was being built nearby. He made the comment, "Why can't they put that plant somewhere else? It will ruin the peace and calm out here." Although no one responded to Walter's remark at the time, one individual from the group later approached the district's board chair, stating, "When we were golfing at the tournament the other day, Walter made a negative comment about the new manufacturing plant being built by the golf course. He must not have known that Mary and Ken, who were in our group, are part owners of the new plant. When we finished our round, they mentioned to me that he should learn to keep his mouth shut!"

As insignificant as this event may have seemed, people will look up to you as a leader in the community. They expect you to use good judgment in everything you do and say in your role as superintendent. It is important to remember that you are "always on the clock" when in public.

Key Point #1: Understand your importance and visibility as the superintendent; be sure to use these components of the position to achieve the district's goals. Keep the following in mind:

- The position comes with an expectation that you will be one of the most visible citizens of the community—if you understand this, you can prepare yourself for the pressures that come with that expectation.

- Since we are in a time where community involvement is on the increase, but there is no consensus about the right way to teach students, you will find yourself at the center of potential debates and emotional discussions. Get ready for those challenges.

- Because of the controversies that exist in even relatively stable districts, understand that you may be dealing with issues that seem trivial or problems that you or your district have not caused. Even if those issues don't seem important to you, they may need to be addressed.

- Find an outlet to occasionally take yourself out of the public eye, even if only for an evening or a couple of days; if you don't, you may find yourself getting tired and even burned out as a result of all of the attention.

- Identify strategies you plan to use to be visible in the community.

As you prepare for the pressures and opportunities that your "visibility" may cause, use the template provided in Figure 1.1 to help you generate ideas and strategies. Once complete, it is advisable to add your Visibility Planning Template as an attachment to your entry plan (Chapter 10).

Once you have completed the template, take some time to reflect on your answers and how they fit into the "public visibility" aspect of being

Figure 1.1 Visibility Planning Template

Consider the following ideas as you begin to think through the issues and challenges that come with your visibility and prominence in the community. Each question/response prompt will help you "flesh out" ideas and opportunities.

1. What strategies or ideas can you employ to identify the necessary level of visibility required in your community?

    _____

    _____

    _____

2. What aspects of your personality are suited to the visibility and prominence demanded of you in the role of superintendent? What aspects of your personality may not be suited to such visibility and importance?

    _____

    _____

    _____

3. How will you maximize the matching portions of your personality while minimizing or compensating for those parts that do not match the visibility portions of the position?

    _____

    _____

    _____

4. How will you gain feedback about your visibility and prominence strategies in relation to your role as superintendent?

    _____

    _____

    _____

5. Once you have gained feedback on your visibility and prominence efforts, how will you make adjustments or refinements in your strategies and ideas?

    _____

    _____

    _____

the superintendent. Decide how your personality fits this requirement and what changes you may need to make in order to be successful. Consider the following questions for personal reflection:

- What did I learn about myself as a result of completing the template?
- What strengths do I presently possess that will help me be successful in this aspect of the superintendency?
- What areas do I need to grow in? How will I gain the information and support for needed growth in these areas?

As we have discussed, visibility in the community and schools is an important issue for new superintendents. Your presence as the community's educational leader will help the public to feel as though you care. In our experience we have found that a visible presence in the community and schools can prevent many pitfalls, which is the subject of the next section. Looking ahead and focusing on ways to prevent missteps is to every superintendent's benefit. In the next section we begin a discussion of this important process.

POTENTIAL PITFALLS FOR NEW SUPERINTENDENTS

Over the years, researchers have conducted studies of the superintendency to examine the unique nature of this job. A study that we found beneficial for our colleagues is highlighted in the book *Becoming a Superintendent: Challenges of School District Leadership*, by Carolyn Hughes Chapman (1997). The book was written based on a research project conducted by twelve professors of educational administration called the Beginning Superintendent Study. During the course of the study, these professors followed eighteen new superintendents, gathering data from a variety of sources.

In addition to the extensive case studies presented on each of the study subjects, the book sums up the collective learning of one part of the research in a chapter entitled "Mistakes Beginning Superintendents Make." Even though we will discuss some of these common mistakes in the sections of this book where they are most closely related, we thought it would be helpful to provide a summarized list.

Keep in mind that these mistakes are the ones made by the new superintendents in the study group. Based on our experiences, they are common to many new superintendents or superintendents new to a district. In subsequent chapters, we will include more details about these common mistakes as they fit into the other problematic areas we are illustrating.

Common New Superintendent Mistakes

- Unshared Vision: Failure to recognize the "human side of the change process" and get stakeholders engaged in helping to determine the direction of the district

- Too Much Too Soon: Too quickly assessing district problems and moving forward without broad understanding or support

- Promises, Promises: Making hasty or baseless promises that worked to compromise credibility

- Offending School Board Members: Not recognizing board members' need to feel important and failing to develop sound working relationships with them

- Not Doing Homework Before Board Meetings: Failing to do the "behind the scenes" work needed to prepare between meetings

- Power Politics: Failing to take time to understand the various power groups and their agendas

- Fickle Loyalties: Not understanding the importance of taking time to get to know all groups before attaching oneself to a particular group

- Failure to Identify Problems: Letting the "status quo" go on too long before beginning to formulate improvement strategies

- Blunt Talk: Forgetting that diplomatic speech may be required when addressing district limitations or problems to avoid alienating people in the district who may have been working under the problematic area

- Alone at the Top: Underestimating the complexity and loneliness of the position

- Hazardous Housecleaning: Undermining trust and credibility by removing practices or personnel without apparent understanding or communication to others

- Overlooking the Obvious: Implementing a very selective course of action to deal with a situation and becoming so focused that an obvious aspect that could more easily work to solve the problem is overlooked

- The High Cost of Saving Money: Instituting measures to save money that end up causing more work and animosity than they are worth (Chapman, 1997)

CHALLENGES OF LEADING A SCHOOL DISTRICT

One of the contextual aspects of being a school superintendent is that, as a result of your importance, visibility, and the amount of community involvement that has entered into the public school arena recently, you will be dealing with a number of constituents who may not see "eye to eye" with you on a variety of issues. In the *Study of the American Superintendency,* authors Glass, Björk, and Brunner (2000) outline this situation in their historical perspective chapter.

In fact, during the 1980s, and to some extent earlier in the 1960s and 1970s, minority groups and school reformers who were unhappy with American public schools often zeroed in on the authority and control held by principals and superintendents. Minority parents and school critics claimed that school administrators (educational experts) who would not, or could not, change the educational system (bureaucracy), obstructed equal educational opportunity and reform (Glass, Björk, & Brunner, 2000, pp. 3–4).

Even though the unhappiness of some community members started several years ago, our experience and work with superintendents show that community members still have issues and look to school boards and superintendents as the people they can give their advice to in the hopes of changing public education in their local communities. Each constituent group may bring to the table different viewpoints, experiences, and paradigms that they use to assess their school system—its successes, challenges, and failures. Some of these opinions are so strong they cause these people to want to take action to help get their viewpoint integrated into the agenda of the school district.

The interests of some community groups may make it difficult for you to maintain your focus on the entire district. However, many of our colleagues over the years have been able to stay on track by spending time focusing on the "Big Picture."

THE IMPORTANCE OF FOCUSING ON THE "BIG PICTURE"

Superintendents new to their positions quickly learn they must develop the ability to view issues from a systemwide perspective (the "big picture"), as well as to understand the minutiae of the organization's operations. This is important if the district is to achieve organizational coherence that will support the accomplishment of its goals. What is the "big picture"? Let's take a few minutes and examine the concept.

The idea of the "big picture" relates to the superintendent's ability to see the total school district (and even the school district community) in the context of day-to-day operations and decisions. As situations arise, it is important to step back and look at the entire system rather than just focus in on one small part of the organization. You may recognize that this concept is very similar to "systems theory" as outlined by author Peter Senge (1989) and others. Let's see how one superintendent used the concept of the "big picture" to deal with a negative situation she faced:

> Deborah entered a school system that had a reputation of being confrontational in the past. Part way into her honeymoon period, the confrontational behaviors started to come out in the various meetings she was attending. She thought about just asserting herself and using the power of her position to squelch the dissention, but instead decided to gather data that would help her see the "big picture" of the problem. She engaged in small group and individual discussions to figure out what could be behind the confrontational behavior. While situations like this can be extremely complex, Deborah found several apparent problems. They included the following:
>
> • A lack of trust among the major groups (employee and external) related to the district
> • A lack of structures for discussion and decision making
> • No clear vehicles to evaluate ideas and move them forward to implementation
>
> Deborah knew that instead of moving forward, she needed to build foundations to help the district and community learn how to work together. She found that there was some interest in looking at Steven Covey's book, *The Seven Habits of Highly Effective People* (Covey, 1989). Even though the book had been published several years ago, she thought it still had a lot of good ideas and strategies that could be very beneficial to the community and the district. She provided support for book discussion groups involving internal and external groups. Once people became more comfortable with the concepts, she operated mixed groups that began making plans using what they had learned in their discussion groups. She also worked with the board to develop a community-based strategic planning process. In addition, Deborah instituted clear agendas for meetings and helped to establish ground rules for discussion.

Even though problems still existed and emerged from time to time, the district began to get a little less confrontational and was able to move forward with several projects. Deborah was very careful to make sure that the district and community did not move too fast initially in order to keep them successful in their quest to improve relations. Her persistence in looking beyond short-term problems or solutions and focusing on the "big picture" helped Deborah improve the school district and community.

Deborah's story may sound too simple to be true, but the attribute that made her a success was her ability to look at the "big picture" rather than focus on small, immediate, and short-term solutions. She knew that until she addressed the foundational problems of the district and community, she would never be able to move them forward in the best interest of students.

As you acclimate into your new superintendency, you will be provided with opportunities each and every day that will test your ability to look at the "big picture." It is a crucial skill for you to have in order to be successful. The template in Figure 1.2 will help you gain the skills necessary to look at the "big picture" as it relates to your district.

Key Point #2: As the superintendent you are expected to be able to see things from the "big picture" or in relation to the best interests of the community. Consider the following as you tackle this challenge:

- Understand that one of the key aspects of your success will be the ability to look at situations in your school district from the "big picture" perspective.

- As people ask for your position on issues, one of the first thoughts that should go through your mind is, "How does this situation impact the entire school district?"

- Begin to communicate the importance of the "big picture" to your board members and your central administrators; eventually, they will begin to think in a similar manner.

- Consider using the strategy "Sticky Note Ripple Effects" from Chapter 8 as you examine issues and decisions.

Figure 1.2 "Big Picture" View Template

This template has been designed to help you think about your district and develop a "big picture" view. Please respond to the following questions/prompts as honestly as possible. After you have completed the template, take a few minutes to look it over and reflect on what you have learned. Superintendents oftentimes find it beneficial to first complete the template on their own and then ask their leadership team complete the process as well. This allows the superintendent to gain a broader perspective on the issues.

1. Describe the context of your district (where is it located, what communities does it encompass, what are its demographics, etc.).

   _____

   _____

   _____

2. What are the issues the district faces? What are the assets the district possesses? What limitations impact the district?

   _____

   _____

   _____

3. Describe the various community groups that reside in the school district. Describe the internal employee groups. What agendas do these groups bring; what seems to make them "tick"? What do they stand to gain from the status quo? What would change for them if the district were to experience reform?

   _____

   _____

   _____

4. Where is the district now in comparison to where it could be? What is preventing it from getting there? What strategies or plans could be implemented to help the district move forward?

   _____

   _____

   _____

JOCKEYING FOR POSITION

Another challenge you may face as a superintendent new to a district is the behavior of some people who "jockey for position" with you. Some new superintendents get the pleasure of meeting people who want to complain about something that happened in the past or with your predecessor. Other people may provide fake or exaggerated compliments to get you on their side. With both of these behaviors, it is tempting to engage in a conversation or even to promise that you will be different, but this is a very dangerous situation you must be prepared to deal with.

Here are several "jockey for position" examples that we have experienced or that have been reported to us in our work with superintendents over the years:

- "We are so glad you're here; it's good to have a superintendent who will listen."
- "Your predecessor was so stubborn; we are hoping that you are more open minded."
- "My neighbor met with you and said you are so open and friendly."
- "Our parent group became frustrated with (name of previous superintendent); we are so glad you will be different."
- "I'm not sure if anyone has mentioned this to you, but there are problems in our district caused by your predecessor; let me tell you about them."
- "This district has great potential but all of our suggestions were ignored by (name of previous superintendent)."
- "We have heard so many good things about you from your previous district."
- "I'm not sure if you understand who your friends and supporters here are; let me tell you."
- "I have a lot of influence here; you can share any problems that you encounter with me and I'll be glad to help you."
- "Many of us in the community have discussed how you will do a much better job than (name of previous superintendent)."

Strategies for dealing with those "jockeying for position":

- Listen to each person fully, but do not make any comments that might be construed as indicating action or commitment.
- When pressed to provide a premature opinion or commitment simply indicate: "I need some time to study the issue, please let me get back to you on this."
- Confirm statements related to the district's culture or operational practice with two or three people prior to formulating an opinion.

- Consult with those who have little to gain prior to considering a significant action, as they will oftentimes provide the most candid feedback.

Keep the following in mind as you encounter negativity related to previous superintendents:

- Anticipate that a negative discussion could come up at almost any meeting you have during your first few months in the district. Try to remember this fact as you meet with each person or group in the district. Just knowing that something negative may be brought up will keep you from getting "blindsided" with an unanticipated issue.
- As you listen to the issue or complaint, work hard to stay open to hearing the core of the message. You may want to jot down the major points that the person sharing this information with you is making.
- Rather than agreeing or disagreeing with the negative allegation or assertion, be ready to use your paraphrasing skills by restating the major parts of the message back to the sender. By restating the major points, you communicate that you are listening—an important attribute of a good superintendent. A more complete description of reflecting skills is included in Chapter 9.
- Resist making judgments or promises related to the issues or complaints. Using your paraphrasing or reflecting skills you can avoid "overpromising." If you do want to make some kind of commitment to the person sharing the complaint, you may be able to commit to checking into the situation then getting back in touch with this person (this technique is similar to the one discussed in the previous section). If you do this be sure to write yourself a reminder and follow through on your promise. If you don't, you'll be the next person on the complaint list.

Key Point #3: Be careful during your initial meetings with employees and constituents so that you don't get trapped, engage in negative conversations, or make unreasonable promises with those whose who may be "jockeying for position."

THE WINDOWPANE MODEL: A TOOL FOR ANALYZING AND UNDERSTANDING CONSTITUENT PERSPECTIVES

As stated earlier, new superintendents must be able to see the "big picture" when considering issues and making decisions. Equally important is the superintendent's ability to analyze and understand varying constituent perspectives. As superintendent it is important to be able to pull back and see things from positions other than your own. You don't have to agree with their perspective, just be able to consider their position so you can understand where they are coming from in relation to the issue at hand.

A visual tool we have used while serving in the position and in our work with superintendents is a "windowpane." Our approach is to ask superintendents to think about their district as if it were a window that contains many smaller panes. Each pane of the window provides a slightly different view if a person stands very close to the window and only looks out of a single pane. When a person stands back and looks out of the entire window (adding together the various small pane views) the picture is complete. As a superintendent you will encounter many groups that are so close to a situation that they can only see it from their small pane. You, on the other hand, should be able to look out the entire window to see the "big picture." At times some of these groups looking through the small windowpanes believe they have full view of the problem, but in reality only see a small part of it. In other words, based upon their experience and knowledge, they can't see through the entire windowpane, but rather just one, or possibly, a few panes. Figure 1.3 illustrates the graphical model we use to explain this idea and Figure 1.4 shows the Windowpane Model with a real example.

Figure 1.3 Windowpane Model

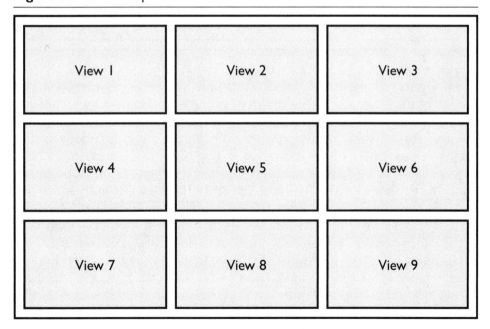

Figure 1.4 Windowpane Model Based on the Content Area of Possibly
Reducing Bus Routes to Save Money in Light of Budget Cuts

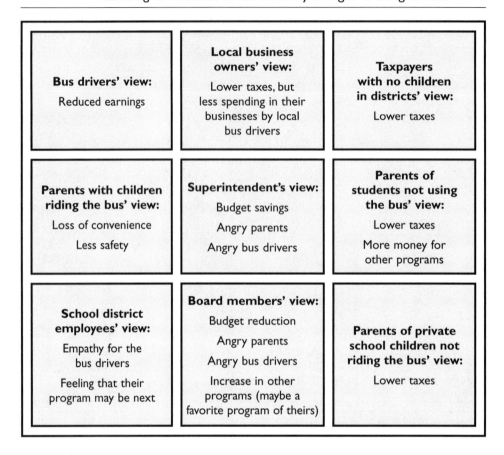

In Figure 1.4 we have identified sample views or perspectives. You
may vary the language or the different groups contained in the windowpanes specific to your circumstances or issues at hand. The focus of the
example is to illustrate how important it is for the superintendent to step
back and view the entire window, including all of the panes, to see how
various ideas or decisions may impact certain groups. Some superintendents have found the graphic so helpful they have used it in their administrative meetings to help them think through their decisions. Once the
various views have been identified, meetings with the groups appearing
in the panes can begin in an effort to address their needs or concerns.

In many cases groups, especially those that are really invested in only
their perspective, simply "don't know what they don't know." Members
of these groups can appear quite harsh at times, believing they understand
the issue and that you are making the "wrong" decision. This is a challenge you are likely to face on a frequent basis. Clearly, if not approached
from an appropriate perspective, these daily encounters can and will lead
to a great deal of frustration on your part.

Key Point #4: It's important for you to be able to "see" the view or perspective of others before you move forward on an idea or plan. Once you have identified their views, you can begin to work to help them see the wider perspective in relation to the idea or plan.

As superintendent you are likely the only one who has achieved the "full view" of a situation. Keeping this concept at the forefront of your mind is of utmost importance in the superintendency. It allows you to set a healthy expectation personally as you deal with issues and challenges. Another byproduct is that you will gain a level of patience and understanding that might not be present without this new perspective. If you always remember that in most situations your challengers will only see through "one pane of the window," it changes how you deal with people, which *is the most important aspect of your position.* You can then probe for areas of misunderstanding or misguided thought and work to correct the errant viewpoints. This process of reflection also allows you to "check" your own viewpoint. Is it possible that you are approaching the issue by looking through only one pane of the window? At times the answer might be yes, but your answer can be modified if you apply this new paradigm of thought in your own decision-making processes.

It is also important to note that at times you will deal with individuals who fully understand the situation at hand, but their priorities may not align with yours or that of the district in general. With any idea or existing practice, someone is benefiting. A change means this benefit is no longer in place. There will undoubtedly be conflict in the decision-making process as people with differing priorities are involved.

Consider the following tips as you deal with constituent perspectives in your superintendency:

- Reflect upon the primary groups you will encounter and develop a sense of the experiences and knowledge they will likely bring to any situation. This will prepare you for the types of questions, comments, and responses you will receive to your proposals and reform efforts.
- Use the Windowpane Model to analyze ideas you wish to propose or when considering an important decision.
- Analyze where you might look through only one pane of the window and challenge yourself to gain an understanding of the "entire window" in that particular area. This process of constant reflection will make you a better superintendent and will aide in the conduct of your work.

THE SUPERINTENDENT AS COMMUNITY LIAISON

Prior to serving in the superintendency some might think the "community liaison" role is lost somewhere in the middle, placed between more pressing and important issues. Although this was never true, today the role of the superintendent as the district's "face in the community" is essential. It is also important to remember that you, as superintendent, are not the only liaison to the community—your administrators and other key personnel are communicating messages as well.

A superintendent should participate in the various service clubs that are available in the community, but be strategic and face this task with clear and focused intention. It is your job to make sure the public receives accurate information about the district and one of the most powerful vehicles for the distribution of these data is to connect with the community's "key communicators." Key communicators are those individuals who influence public opinion in your community. He or she may be an elected official, but could be an employee at the local grocery store. The point is that your district's key communicators will likely come from both the traditional and hidden leadership structures of the community. Your task is to identify these individuals and determine how to best communicate with each one, as the relationship you build will pay tremendous dividends when the community's support is required.

As the district's community liaison the superintendent should develop "strategic discussion points" which will ensure that a purposeful message is getting out to the community's key communicators (as well as others). One of the strongest ways to combat the influence of misinformation campaigns and develop confidence in the school system is to drive home over a period of time, via the most respected individuals in the community, a message you want every household to understand about the district. This concept is successful because it preempts the work of those who would like to promote negativity about the district. In essence, this is the process of developing "sound bites" about the district. These messages should be simple, short, and extremely memorable. Your goal with this effort is to ultimately hear members of the community echoing the messages, which you are sharing over and over again with the district's key communicators. Once the district's sound bites are the community's mantra about its school system, you will know that you have succeeded in your efforts.

In a district where one of the authors served as superintendent he was blessed to experience academic performance in the top 5 percent and expenditures in the bottom 10 percent, as compared to other districts statewide. This message was communicated on every possible occasion:

"Our schools perform in the top 5 percent, while spending is in the bottom 10 percent." This key message communicated that constituents of the district received good results for a relatively low level of investment—a good value. The message was broadly shared in verbal and written communications across the community and eventually, over time, the superintendent began to hear it coming back to him. It had an impact on the way the community viewed its school district and how they chose to describe it to others.

> **Key Point #5:** Understand your role in serving as a community liaison. In this role you will function as a sort of conduit between the community and the school district.

Even though we will discuss communication in more depth in Chapter 9, it is important now that you begin to think about a process to identify the key communicators in your district.

DEVELOP A KEY COMMUNICATORS LIST

Identifying key communicators can be accomplished by asking for input from board members, existing district administrators, key community members, and others to help identify the district's most influential people in a few important categories. These categories may be slightly different in each district but could include business leadership, PTA leaders, parents, key employees, and so on.

The key communicator categories should lead to the identification of your district's power base. It should be noted that as you progress through this process you may not find key communicators in each major area, or it is possible that a key communicator will be identified across several areas. Neither of these issues is a problem, but rather opportunities to better understand your community. If only a few key communicators are identified, then you have fewer individuals to focus on regarding your communication efforts. If one individual shows up in numerous groups this indicates that they might be more influential than others who are identified in the process. Figure 1.5 contains a matrix showing the typical categories and potential members of each for school districts.

Figure 1.5 Key Communicator Identification Matrix

Potential Key Communicator Areas*	Method of Identification	Communication Methods for Identified Groups	Potential Members of the Group
Elected Officials	• Studying school district's list of municipalities, counties, and other jurisdictions	• Individual monthly meetings • Joining groups which provide access to these individuals • Periodic e-mail updates regarding district's activities	• School board • Other elected officials • School employees • Community members
Service Clubs and Organizations	• Community guides • School board • District employees • Community members	• Periodic reports to the organization • Annual "State of the Schools" presentations • Attendance at meetings	• Same as shown in Methods of Identification section
Athletic Organizations	• District coaches • District athletic director • Community members	• Attendance at meetings • Periodic e-mail communications regarding district's athletic issues/needs • Development of an "Athletic Advisory Council"	• Same as shown in Methods of Identification section
Business Community	• Chamber of Commerce • Rotary • School board • Other service clubs	• Attendance at identified meetings • "Special events" for business community through the district • Periodic, business issue related print or e-mail communications	• Business leaders • School board • Chamber executive
Religious Community	• Ministerial associations • Community guides	• Periodic attendance at ministerial meetings • District-sponsored events for clergy	• School board • Community members

*This list of potential key communicator groups is not exhaustive, but is meant to serve as guide in the identification process. Superintendents can probe school board members and others to determine which individuals and community groups require identification in their particular district.

This section focused on the fact that the superintendent is the district's "community liaison." In this day and age of increased "no vote" efforts and public scrutiny, it is of vital importance that the district establish a strong relationship with the community. As superintendent it is your job to lead this effort, keeping close tabs on what residents of the district think and feel about their schools. It is important to identify the district's key communicators and engage them frequently. To do so establishes relationships, which ultimately should lead to trust. Clearly they will hear a message about the school district; the question is *what* will they hear and *whom* will they hear it from? Furthermore, when a tax initiative is proposed will you, as superintendent, have enough relationship capital with the community's key communicators that they will trust what the district is saying? To conclude these thoughts, contemplate the words of Peter Drucker, the influential management consultant and university professor, who said: "The best way to predict the future is to create it!"

Consider the following tips as you serve as community liaison in your district:

- You are the face of the school district in everything you say, everything you do, and in every interaction in which you are engaged. Don't ever underestimate the fact that the impression you leave will have an impact on your tenure in the superintendency. Always be friendly, positive, and helpful regardless of the situation.
- Be cognizant of the fact that other district employees (key administrators and other staff members) are also liaisons with the community. Be sure these individuals are clear regarding what should be consistently communicated to the public.
- Know your district's hidden and formal leadership structures and make an effort to strategically focus the district's communication points on the key communicators in your district.
- Do not underestimate the benefit of strategic communication points and the fact that you need to be purposeful in making sure the district's message is spread with intention and perseverance.

THE CHANGING ROLE OF THE SUPERINTENDENCY

The role of the superintendent has changed dramatically over the years. Once a position many aspired to in school systems—a role with tremendous influence and long tenure—it has now changed, especially in urban settings. Is this change for better, or worse? We each must judge this question for ourselves as reforms in the position can be viewed as both positive and negative. Consider the words of Susan Moore Johnson, author of *Leading to Change: The Challenge of the New Superintendency* (1996) and former academic dean and professor of education in administration, planning, and social policy at the Harvard Graduate School of Education:

> In the past, the job was primarily a managerial position. Now, a different approach to leadership is needed to tackle educational and political issues simultaneously. Some of those challenges are well beyond the superintendent's control or influence, and many of them require substantial financial investments that society is not prepared to make. (Johnson, 1996)

In the past it was clear that the superintendent was to establish financial stability, oversee the physical plant, maintain well-disciplined schools, and ensure each child had a textbook. Today, we are in a new era that continues to be redefined as time progresses. In this new era a completely different skill set is required for the position of superintendent. Although the position still requires managerial expertise and awareness of the district's day-to-day operations, it has become much more oriented toward leading, setting direction, and holding the organization accountable for results.

NAVIGATING THE CHANGING LANDSCAPE

In our opinion, as we progress into the future and the landscape for superintendents' changes, there are at least three basic ideas which superintendents must understand to achieve success. These three ideas are not meant to be all encompassing, but rather to point out issues which will require tremendous levels of thought and finesse. These include:

1. Successful change cannot be mandated (Fullan, 2001); it requires organizational support.
2. Superintendents must know which hill to "die on." In other words, they recognize the decisions that are so important they would stake their job on the proper resolution of these issues.
3. Superintendents must understand the components of successful communication.

New superintendents should quickly understand and gain appreciation for the fact that they are as close to serving in an elected role as possible. They serve at the pleasure of the local school board. In today's changing environments, most are one election away from a potentially hostile board. More and more superintendents are becoming facilitators of their boards and community constituent groups. Let's look at the three previously mentioned basic ideas and how they relate to the changing landscape of the school superintendency.

Successful School Change

It is human nature for leaders to desire to "win" the competition. This is the way they are wired, and their tenacity likely signals the reason for their success. How this translates to the superintendency is that you need to realize major change requires organizational support; you can't plan it and organize it on your own. Although this sounds self-evident, superintendents in most cases fail with major initiatives because they either don't involve others, or do so in a cursory manner. John Kotter, in *Leading Change: Emotional Aspects of the Change Process* (1996), indicates that major change must start with stirring the organization's emotions. Successful leaders figure out how to get this done (see Kotter's book for examples) so that a large portion of the organization is ready for change prior to introducing a new initiative. This process can be compared to preparing a garden. We must first spend significant time following a number of individual steps to prepare the soil for successful germination of the seeds. Organizations are no different; a great idea or needed change effort can't be simply sprung on the system without first preparing everyone for the new initiative. This is not a couple of speeches and a report identifying reasons for change, but potentially a yearlong, multifaceted process. We speak to the change process in greater depth in Chapter 5, but it is important to realize finesse in this area is a prerequisite for the effective superintendent.

> **Key Point #6:** Understand the attributes of effective change before attempting to move new initiatives or plans forward. This is an idea that will help you transcend a changing school landscape.

Hills to "Die On"

Even though the superintendency is normally a physically safe job, successful superintendents learn quickly about the concept of identifying which hills to "die on." This war-related term has been used by many of the colleagues we have worked with over the years to indicate the issues that the superintendent stakes his or her professional reputation and survival on in the school district. This is an issue of tremendous importance as it speaks to where, as superintendent, you should take a stand in the decision making process. During the course of your career, from the earliest stages through the length of your tenure, you will be faced with this dilemma.

The challenge is that in many serious situations there isn't a clear answer to the problem. When you think about it, this makes sense as it wouldn't truly be a decision if the correct path were clear! To effectively navigate the political reality of when and how to make a decision, you will need to work from a solid decision making base. What does this mean? It simply indicates that you need to clearly search your soul for what your philosophy is in making decisions when the going gets tough. Do you take the side of the most influential board member, staff member, or community representative? Do you sacrifice individual employees to keep others happy? Do you use politically acceptable platitudes such as "it's in the best financial interest of the district"? We mention these questions as, unfortunately, some of your colleagues will take such a path to keep the peace, or save their job. Our experience tells us that the very best superintendents develop a few Decision-Making Tenets that they operate from when the going gets tough. These tenets become their guiding light—their lighthouse in the fog, if you will—as tough situations are faced. There is never a shortage of situations in the superintendency that require political and/or decision-making courage, and those who operate from a set of predetermined tenets always find themselves to be at greater peace when the dust settles.

Below we have provided a matrix that leads you through the process of developing your own set of Decision-Making Tenets.

Decision-Making Tenets Development Matrix

Step #1: Develop your educational philosophy (put this in writing). If you have completed this exercise in the past, use this opportunity to revisit your previous thinking. If this is the first occasion for you to develop a written philosophy, be honest with yourself. You may check your thoughts with close colleagues or your spouse to determine whether your ideas are truly reflective of who you are and how you operate.

Items to Spur Thought

- What does the phrase "all kids can learn" mean to you?

- Do you truly focus on the students, or do you defer to adults and the culture in the school system? Why or why not?

- What do you believe about student assessment and progress monitoring (formative and summative)?

- To what extent are parents responsible for student performance?

Step #2: Distill your educational philosophy down to a few items that represent your focus; your hills to "die on" (Tenets).

Items to Spur Thought

- Do these items represent issues you feel deeply about in your heart and soul?

- Is there a solid base of research that supports your philosophy?

- Can you easily articulate these Tenets of your philosophy and debate them if possible? Are they memorable?

- Do you comprehensively understand the opposing view?

- To what extent would you stand on these issues? Would you stake your job on these items? Would you hold true to them unless the board indicates you should change your mind?

Step #3: Develop a written list of these Tenets and post them in your office.

Items to Spur Thought

- If asked, how will you describe these Tenets to others? What is their purpose?

- Did you choose items that strike you at the core of your being, or did you opt for those you believe are less controversial (there is no right or wrong answer here, but rather what you can truly live with individually)?

- Do you feel comfortable operating from these Tenets when the going gets tough?

Step #4: Design a plan to revisit these Tenets at an annual individual retreat where you spend time alone in reflection.

Items to Spur Thought

- Do you believe your Tenets can change over time with maturation and new data?

- How do you plan to record thoughts related to your Tenets throughout the year (keep a file, a journal, etc.)?

- Did you face decisions that challenged your Tenets during the year? How did you react? Did you hold true, or did you take a different path?

Key Point #7: Identify the principles that provide the foundation for your ideas and opinions. Be able to clearly and concisely share them related to the major decisions you will face. Don't "dig in" on issues over stubbornness, but do take a stand when an issue is directly related to one of your core foundational values.

Successful Communicator

The next skill that adept superintendents must master to transcend a changing landscape is that of successful communicator. Today's superintendent must become an expert at communicating with a range of constituents using skills that fit a particular context. Although most people equate a good communicator with a "good public speaker," we believe this is only one of many items you must have in your toolbox.

Effective communicators are masters of written and nonverbal communication as well. Most of us can identify an individual who we think of as a "good communicator." In most cases these individuals are seen as articulate, friendly, outgoing, and willing to listen. Although these skills may be consistent with our "vision" of a good communicator, successful communicators come in a number of different packages.

As we think about the position of superintendent, it is true that you are periodically engaged in large group verbal communication, but superintendents are also called upon to communicate frequently in writing—memos, e-mails, newsletters—and in small groups. To be successful in these endeavors you must become an "effective" verbal and written communicator. Also, good communication is considered two-way, which means the superintendent not only has to send good communication but must receive as well. Effective two-way communication skills in multiple areas can be achieved through practice, further study, or gaining assistance from others when needed. Superintendents must not only be effective verbal and written communicators, but they must master small group and nonverbal communication strategies.

Superintendents spend much of each day in small group meetings or engaged with individuals. When they walk down the hall or greet others, their every move is being watched by someone. Employees, community members, and parents will likely engage the superintendent very infrequently and thus an initial impression goes a long way.

Regarding small groups, it is imperative that superintendents become expert facilitators. The methods they employ while facilitating a small group can leave the group feeling honored, or upset. Again, superintendents are leaders and they want to verbalize their agenda, and many times this comes at the expense of broad-based group participation. Expert small group facilitation represents a cache of skills that are mastered and used by successful superintendents. To further your skills in this area we recommend reading *Effective Group Facilitation in Education: How to Energize Meetings and Manage Difficult Groups,* by Dr. John Eller (2004). Dr. Eller outlines a number of strategies that will prepare you to expertly facilitate the numerous small groups you will encounter during your tenure as a superintendent.

Nonverbal communication is a topic we seldom consider as superintendents, but one that holds great importance. Often defined as gestures, signs, and body cues; it has been said that approximately 90 percent of your communication is carried through nonverbal means. Thus, when you are interacting with people—sitting in a meeting, listening to someone's comments, thoughts, or ideas—90 percent of what you communicate comes through your actions, expressions, posture, etc. Powerful information! Nonverbal communication can be broken into three primary parts: (1) the items you can do nothing about—your gender, race, age, or height; (2) the items you can, with effort, change—your dress, hair, or weight; and finally, (3) the items you already have that you can choose to use—gesture, eye contact, voice, and so on. Superintendents who make an effort to say "hi" in the hallway, place their hand on someone's shoulder and thank them for a job well done, or smile and make eye contact with a parent at the grocery store are typically seen as friendly, open, and engaged.

Figure 1.6 outlines some nonverbal communication skills and their potential impact on others. As you review it, think about how you might use these ideas as you connect with others in your particular district. Remember it is likely the small, seemingly insignificant interactions that take place on a daily basis will define for people who you are as a leader.

> **Key Point #8:** As you begin your superintendency, keep effective communication strategies at the forefront of your most important behaviors. Be sure to think about effective two-way communication and the integration of spoken, written, and nonverbal methods in your tool kit.

Consider the following tips as you think about the changing role of the superintendency:

- First, realize the superintendency will continue to change, but what won't change is that the role will continue to require an individual who can lead but not forget the importance of the day-to-day operation.

Figure 1.6 Nonverbal Communication Skills and Their Potential Impact on Others

Communication Skill	Improvement Efforts	Application
Smiling	• Focus on smiling when interacting with people or simply walking down the hall.	• Smiling provides impression of confidence, approachability, energy.
Posture/Body Orientation	• Stand erect, but not rigid. • Lean forward slightly when talking to others. • Don't slouch.	• Standing erect shows energy and confidence. • Leaning forward, especially when introducing yourself, will display interest and respect.
Proximity	• Close proximity can show engagement and interest. • Develop awareness of how to assess a person's comfort level with your proximity.	• Use proximity as a tool to show that you are actively listening. • Recognize the signs of proximity discomfort: movement away, eye aversion, leg swaying, tapping.
Paralinguistics	• Understand various aspects of speech: tone, pitch, loudness, inflection, etc.	• Use aspects of speech to make a point, indicate interest, or signal concern.
Appropriate Touch	• On occasion use appropriate touch to show concern, caring, or interest.	• Use appropriate touch to add emphasis to your message.

- Become a student of the change process and read all you can regarding its successful implementation. Change will be the one constant throughout your career.
- Take the time to assess and understand your educational philosophy, as it will become the foundation from which to operate. Your philosophy should be distilled down to a few Decision-Making Tenets, which need to be revisited on an annual basis.
- Put in the effort to become an "effective" verbal and written communicator, but become an expert at small group facilitation and nonverbal communication.

SUMMARY

Now that it's official and you have the job, it's important for you to really understand the nature of the position you have accepted. This chapter was developed as a way for you to see the historical context of the superintendency, some of the roles and expectations of the job, and the changing landscape of the position. It was also designed to provide you with some ideas and strategies and to give you a chance to think and process how you will move forward and make the job a successful venture for you and a quality investment for the district you serve. As you reflect on your new position, think about the following:

- What are the major expectations the community has for me in relation to my visibility as the superintendent?
- What lessons can I learn from the research related to mistakes new superintendents make?
- How can I identify the key communicators in my district?
- How can I use the Windowpane Model to understand the different perspectives groups hold in the school community? Once I know these, how do I need to move forward?
- What foundational skills and behaviors can I count on to help me be successful as the landscape of the district and the superintendency changes?

The job of school superintendent is both challenging and rewarding. It will provide you with untold professional stimulation, as well as many very frustrating moments. One key relationship that needs to be established and maintained is the relationship between the board and the superintendent. In Chapter 2, The Superintendent–School Board Relationship: A Cornerstone of Your Success, you will learn how to make this crucial relationship work for you.

2

The Superintendent–
School Board Relationship

A Cornerstone of Your Success

It seemed rather incongruous that in a society of super-sophisticated communication, we often suffer from a shortage of listeners.

—Erma Bombeck

E d, a seasoned superintendent of fifteen years, realized that his relationship with the board was going sour. It started with a negative evaluation in May and as winter approached board members were attacking him in board meetings regarding "poor communication and not doing his homework." The board claimed that without proper information it couldn't make decisions that were in the best interest of the students, staff, and community. One board member in particular accused Ed of "withholding" information in an effort to control the board. This board member went on to claim that Ed communicated with those who agreed with his philosophy and withheld data from those who desired to hold him accountable.

Does this sound familiar? Unfortunately, superintendents can often become victims of a poor relationship with their boards in the absence of purposeful planning. It sneaks up on them and before they know it, their job is on the line. As a new superintendent you will need to work hard to develop and maintain a good relationship with your board members, which oftentimes is a function of effective superintendent–board communication.

ABOUT THIS CHAPTER

This chapter will focus on the relationship between you and your board, ways to start off on the right foot, and strategies and ideas to continue to build on your relationship as your superintendency unfolds. As you read the information in this chapter, pay particular attention to the following:

- The importance of "equal treatment" when working with board members
- The uniqueness of the superintendent–board chair/president relationship
- The basics of developing an initial relationship with your board members
- Strategies for addressing normal and emergency communications with the board
- Board standards and operating protocols

Keep your individual needs in mind as you review this chapter as well. Remember each district, board, and superintendent is different. Since your district and situation is unique, your success is based on the needs of your board and the strengths you possess as the school district leader. Carefully evaluate the strategies presented and select the ones that make the most sense for you and your situation.

MANAGING THE SUPERINTENDENT– BOARD RELATIONSHIP

Strategies used to develop and sustain healthy, long-lasting relationships with school boards are manyfold. Most correlate to aspects of effective communication and therefore this is where we will spend the bulk of our time. We believe that relationships are likely most significantly impacted, positively or negatively, by the quality of the communication that takes place among the parties. In considering the nuances of managing the superintendent–board relationship we have identified two areas that are of vital importance:

- Equal treatment of your board members
- Superintendent–board president/chair interaction

THE IMPORTANCE OF EQUAL TREATMENT

Equal treatment of board members is the first lesson new superintendents must learn. A good time to concentrate on this concept with your board is at the very beginning of your superintendency. This time is commonly known as the "honeymoon" period where everyone is happy and communication seems easy. Normally you are not being bombarded with complex issues during this period and can work on the relationship. Slowly, as the year progresses, you may begin to establish relationships, receive requests, make decisions, or run into issues that put you in a precarious position with individual board members. As your tenure continues, if you are not purposeful in your approach, you may develop "allies" on the board as well as "detractors." If you have not addressed these issues up front during your "honeymoon" period, you could be headed for trouble.

Since many new superintendents worked as principals or central office administrators before assuming the superintendency, they have only reported to one supervisor during most of their career. During the superintendent preparation process there was likely little, if any, training related to how one deals with establishing an effective board relationship. All of a sudden the new superintendent is serving a board that is charged with acting as one, but is really a group of individuals with different expectations, demands, and personalities. Individuals new to the superintendency must be aware of this job challenge and have a plan for establishing and sustaining an effective relationship with their board.

Board members themselves are often times not well prepared for this part of their role either. Even though board members in most states receive some training, they likely did not spend much time on the superintendent–board relationship or the impact of making individual demands. This may be the first time some of these individuals have served on a board of directors, and they are often pulled in competing directions as a result of the public involvement in education we talked about in Chapter 1. They may not have strategies for dealing with these constituent demands and want you, as superintendent or your staff, to be conducting individual research for them on a regular basis. The question is, how do you deal with these situations when they arise? How do you provide appropriate service to your board without showing favoritism or serving one member's needs over that of another?

In our work with superintendents and through our own experience in the position we have observed two significant ways in which equal treatment of board members can become a problem for the new superintendent. Although we will speak to each in greater depth below, the first relates to superintendents showing deference to particular individuals on the board, in essence developing an "inner circle." The second condition focuses on how the superintendent deals with individual board member requests for information and time.

The "Inner Circle"

In our observation superintendents develop an "inner circle" of board members over time and typically without intention. These individual board members may be people the superintendent holds in high regard, or who are seen as prominent in the community. Superintendents tend to often agree with these board members and the board members tend to fully support the superintendent's initiatives. It is human nature to connect more frequently with those who we trust or feel support our initiatives. If we don't feel support from a board member, or if there is clear opposition, we, as human beings, will seek the refuge of those we perceive to be on our side. This tendency is both natural and dangerous. New superintendents don't typically start out intending to fall into this trap, but subtly, over time, as individual relationships build, it can happen. It may be that the superintendent has a special connection to a board member because of a common interest, or the board member may be highly complimentary of the superintendent's performance. Regardless, the condition can develop and its impact is often negative and dramatic. Not unlike the employee who observes favoritism taking place in their environment, board members will become aware of this state as well. Once this happens the superintendent's objectivity is compromised and his or her decisions are questioned. Board members on the outside of the "inner circle" will consider the superintendent's motive when decisions are made or initiatives are supported. Again, as subtle and unintentional as this condition may feel to the superintendent, it is deadly to his or her relationship with the remainder of the board.

Addressing Individual Board Member Requests

School board members have backgrounds that are typically as diverse as the constituents they serve. Some will be retired community members who have time to thoroughly consume each board packet and communication from the district, while others will be individuals who oftentimes arrive at the board meeting late having just arrived home from a business trip. What this diversity means for you as superintendent is that some board members may be heavily involved in their work, calling you on a daily basis, while others will only contact you in case of emergency. The important part to understand is that you will receive individual board member requests for information or time, but how you address those requests is pivotal to your success in maintaining a solid relationship with your entire board. What we have observed to be most effective in addressing this issue is to let your board know up front when you receive individual requests for information or time so that those requests and any accompanying data will be distributed to all. This has a threefold effect: (1) it curbs individual requests which board members might make without the knowledge of their colleagues; (2) it establishes "equal treatment" of all board members; and (3) it has the impact of reducing unmanageable requests which might take extensive time and effort by you or your staff.

Armed with knowledge of these potential pitfalls as a new superintendent, you can properly establish norms with your board early on. We spoke to addressing these issues during your "honeymoon period" and frankly, the earlier the better. Our experience is that these behaviors, especially individual board requests, will begin early on in your tenure and the sooner you develop a protocol for their resolution the sooner you can begin to establish a healthy superintendent–board relationship.

Key Point #1: Be aware of the fact that how you interact with individual board members and respond to their requests will set the stage for how you are perceived. Take care to establish patterns of equal treatment with your board.

Strategies to ensure equal treatment of all board members include the following:

- Monitor the attention and time you provide to your board members.
- Be overt about your goal to provide equal attention to board members; set a goal with your members and periodically revisit the goal to see how you are doing.
- Gather the perceptions of your board members through interviews and surveys to see if you are providing equal attention and communication to them.
- Ask your board president to talk with board members and gain their perceptions about the time you are spending with them; meet with your board president and talk about what he or she is learning as a result of these discussions.
- Remind board members about your feeling on the importance of equal treatment; ask them to provide you with feedback about your efforts and the strategies you have implemented.

Putting one or more of these strategies in place will help ensure you are treating all your board members in a similar manner. In the initial stages of your superintendency, you may find that a good way to ensure equal treatment is to communicate with each board member using the same methods. After you have become more established, you may find that doing the same thing for each member may not be to your benefit. Let's look at another side of equal treatment.

WHEN IS EQUAL TREATMENT UNEQUAL?

You will find that providing equal time and attention to each board member will work in the short term, but as your relationship evolves you'll see each board member has slightly different needs, and you'll want to consider their specific needs as you continue to work with them. While this may be challenging, your treatment should *equally* meet the needs of all your board members. Let's see how Juanita started to meet the needs of her board members in the area of communication:

> Juanita started her superintendency by working hard to make sure she provided each board member with equal time and equal information. As her relationship with them grew, she started to see that they had different levels of need. She met with each board member individually to find out what their needs were, and then began to change her strategies to better meet those needs.
>
> Initially, she was calling her board chair on a daily basis and the other members on a weekly basis. Antonio, one of her board members, told her that she did not need to call as he could obtain his information from the Friday Update and the board packet. Jennifer, another board member, told Juanita that she too preferred not to receive a call.
>
> Juanita normally delivered the weekly board informational packet personally to each member. Some of the board members wanted their packet delivered to their place of employment, while others preferred to have it delivered to their home. Juanita normally delivered the packet on Thursday afternoons. One board member explained to Juanita that he was normally out of town on Thursdays, so she could mail the packet to him since he wouldn't be able to review it until the weekend.
>
> As Juanita made these changes she kept in contact with the members to make sure her efforts were working for them. In the end she met board members' needs but she did not do everything exactly the same for each board member. By meeting their needs and constantly monitoring her efforts, she was able to get high marks for her communication efforts with her board.

Keep in mind that Juanita's success was based on her ability to find out her board members' needs, and then design strategies to meet those needs. She also assessed her situation to make sure her ideas would work. Meeting individual needs can be a complex task, but well worth the effort. Ideas to guide you as you work to meet your board members' needs include:

- When working to meet board member needs in the areas of attention and communication, remember that you want to make sure each member feels equally important and informed.
- Before thinking about varying your techniques for board members, be sure you have established a good base of attention and information.
- Talk with your board members continuously to make sure your efforts are working for each and every one of them.
- If you begin to perceive that a member is feeling less important or less informed, find out the issue and make the necessary adjustments.

Key Point # 2: Consider the unique needs of individual board members when working to provide them with "equal treatment and information."

SUPERINTENDENT–BOARD CHAIR/PRESIDENT INTERACTION

In most districts, if it is not recognized as policy, it is definitely part of the culture for the board chair/president to assume an elevated role from the other board members. After all, the chair or president of the board is seen as a leadership role within the board structure. This role may be clearly defined or more informal. One item that seems to be consistent across districts is that the superintendent is required to meet with the board chair/president regarding development of the board meeting agenda. Additionally, superintendents will, in most cases, informally communicate with the board chair/president regarding other topics of importance. Although, as mentioned in the previous section, it is important to communicate equally with all board members, by nature of the position you will communicate more frequently with the board chair/president. As such it is important to develop a separate set of communication standards for your interactions with this person.

The board chair/president may serve as a sounding board to the superintendent for district initiatives, or provide the superintendent with guidance regarding communication with other board members. It is important to get clarity regarding the role of the chair/president during your initial meetings (or retreat) with the board. For your protection it should also be clear how the entire board "views" the relationship between the superintendent and the board chair/president. What powers are delegated to the chair/president by the board? What should be communicated to the entire board and what is communicated individually to the chair/president?

From our experiences, some new superintendents do not clarify this relationship and then fall victim to mismatched expectations. The most common problems involve other board members not believing in the leadership abilities of the chair/president and wanting to be more involved in the leadership of the board. Their issues with the board chair/president put the superintendent in the middle of a power struggle. The superintendent needs to help the board work through this kind of issue as their mediator, or utilize the services of an outside facilitator.

Another common problem we have seen is that one or more board members wants to "micro-manage" the operations of the district. These board members want all of the attention and informational details normally reserved for the superintendent–chair/president relationship. This is another situation that requires intervention to get members back on track.

Key Point #3: Do not leave role expectations with your board chair/president to chance. Assist the board in identifying/clarifying this important role and your responsibilities in the working relationship.

Establishing Superintendent–Board Chair/President Interaction Norms

The initial expectations for your interaction patterns with the board chair/president may come from the board chair/president or other board members as well. You need to take the initial ideas and make sure all of the board members are involved in the final product. Conducting an open discussion with the entire board regarding the president's role and your relationship with him or her is a must. Most superintendents hold this discussion as part of the formal, open agenda. This provides a formal record of the discussion and ensures clear understanding of the expectations for everyone.

It is important to also remember that, especially for a newly elected board chair/president, they may not realize the importance of clarifying their role in relation to other board members. One of the greatest areas of tension between board members comes in the form of a mistrust that begins with individual members feeling they are not included in the communication loop. It is incumbent upon you as a new superintendent to make sure this issue is addressed once a new board chair/president is elected. The same role clarification is crucial for boards that either may not have had the discussion in the past or for a board that may be dysfunctional in their formal operations.

Strategies for helping your board understand the importance of role clarification include the following:

- Use the consultant from the search firm that assisted in your placement to conduct a seminar with your board.
- Provide informational articles highlighting the importance of the clarification of the board chair/president role in relation to the board and superintendent.
- Meet informally with the board chair/president and board members to help them understand the importance of role clarification.
- Use a consultant from the state school board association to explain the importance of clarifying the board chair/president's relationship with the board and the superintendent.
- Use a member from another board that has credibility with your board to explain the importance of role.

Keeping the Chair/President Relationship Productive

The superintendent–board chair/president relationship is one that demands considerable attention, time, and effort. In the following lists are productive strategies to both establish and maintain the relationship, as well as potential pitfalls that should be avoided.

Strategies for successful superintendent–board chair/president interaction include the following:

- Determine the frequency of communication desired by the board chair/president.
- Develop a standard related to when the board chair/president should be contacted regarding important situations/information.
- Contact the board chair/president in advance of developing the board agenda.
- Gain an understanding early of how the board views the role of the chair/president.
- Assist the board chair/president in developing and adopting tools for board self-evaluation.
- Be willing to serve as a sounding board for the board chair/president.

- Provide the board chair/president with ideas related to the superintendent evaluation process.
- Remember to always introduce the board chair/president when jointly attending meetings.

Pitfalls to avoid regarding superintendent–board chair/president interaction include the following:

- Forgetting to contact the board chair/president first when serious issues arise.
- Usurping the board chair/president's authority when making decisions, or dealing with the district's various publics.
- Failing to place the board chair/president (and other board members) in a position of importance when announcing district successes.
- Handling calls from board members related to board member conflict; rather, always refer these issues to the board chair/president.
- Engaging in negative gossip with the board chair/president about other board members.
- Taking action on an issue which the board chair/president promotes without the full involvement of the board.

The superintendent–board chair/president relationship is one of the most vital you will establish during your tenure. Most seasoned superintendents indicate that they talk with their board chair/president on a daily basis, therefore establishing a successful relationship from the beginning is of clear importance. As stated earlier, it is also significant to understand how the board corporately views the role of the chair/president and his or her interaction with the superintendent. Successful superintendents define these factors early with their boards, and thus enhance ongoing communication and trust.

> **Key Point #4:** Keep in mind that the individual you will speak with most in the district is the board chair/president. Understand the complexity of this unique relationship and take the necessary steps to ensure success.

THE BASICS OF BOARD COMMUNICATION

Sound and effective communication between the superintendent and the board is the foundation of a good relationship. In the Beginning Superintendent Study (BSS) mentioned in Chapter 1 (Gordon, in Chapman, 1997), a mistake made by many new superintendents was offending school board members and not doing homework between board meetings. The authors provided a list of "offending behaviors" and "board meeting homework problems." They include

- recommending personnel actions involving staff that had special, long-term relationships with board members;
- being too optimistic about potential program implementation or not being completely honest about district problems;
- not paying close enough attention to the meaning and implications of board member voting patterns; board members who were outvoted sometimes represented major community groups and their wishes;
- failure to recognize the implications one negative vote and the lack of consensus had on a decision; the board member became alienated;
- failure of the superintendent to "equally inform" all board members related to issues and decisions;
- insufficient communication with board members between meetings;
- bringing new ideas forward in public board meetings without extensive discussion in advance with board members;
- lack of clarity regarding the roles of the superintendent and board chair/president, resulting in a poor relationship. (Gordon, in Chapman, 1997, p. 200)

Although avoiding all of these problems sounds intuitive, the devil is in the details regarding how the superintendent achieves a positive working relationship with his or her board. The bottom line is that the quality of the superintendent-board relationship is strongly correlated with the clarity and frequency of communication between the parties. Many of our colleagues report they spend a significant portion of their time each week in communication with their board members. Since the superintendency is a position that deals with an overwhelming number of people and amount of information in a given day, it is crucial that a plan for superintendent–board communication be developed as early as possible in your tenure. How is this plan developed? Normally, superintendents new to a district talk with their board chair/president and with individual board members in defining an effective communication plan. We recommend four basic components of the communication plan, which will be outlined as the chapter proceeds. These four areas are as follows:

o   What form of communication does each board member individually prefer?

    o   Determine the forms of communication and frequency of contact you will use to keep the board informed.

    o   Outline the role of the board chair/president in the communication process.

    o   Establish standards that outline when board members will be contacted regarding emergency situations.

Let's see how one superintendent worked with her board to identify their informational needs and developed a communication plan:

> Mary knew her board would want to have input into her communication plan. When she was hired, the board chair told the rest of the members that he would take charge of her initial orientation since she was starting in the summer and several board members would be in and out of town during this time period. Mary took advantage of the extended time her board chair was giving her and talked with him about his communication needs. As he talked, Mary took notes on a white board in her office. She reviewed these notes with her chair for clarity. She developed a draft of her communication plan for superintendent–board interactions.
>
> Once she completed this task, she called individual board members and invited them to meet with her to gain perspective about their communication needs. She took notes and used these thoughts to refine her communication plan. She distributed her plan one final time to obtain board member feedback, made adjustments, and then brought the plan to the entire board for their eventual adoption.

Since Mary spent time up front working with her board to determine their needs, she has a clear understanding of their expectations regarding her communication with them. However, Mary normally goes one step further and communicates more than the board expects. She ascribes to the saying, "Underpromise and overdeliver." This belief pays big dividends for her with her board. On her yearly evaluation, she gets good ratings for her ability to communicate.

Key Point #5: The most important relationship you will need to nurture is the one between you and your board; you will need to put together a purposeful communication plan to build this relationship.

Since a high level of communication between a new superintendent and his or her board members is so crucial, and since many new superintendents are not accustomed to this high level of communication, we have provided a planning template in Figure 2.1. Use this template or adapt it to fit your unique needs.

Figure 2.1   Board Communication Analysis Template

This template has been designed to assist you as you begin to diagnose the general communication needs of your board. Think about the board as a whole when completing this template. Use the results of board member interviews, discussions with district staff, and a review of board minutes when answering the questions below.

1. How active does this board seem in the operation of the school district?

_____

_____

_____

2. What methods did the previous superintendent use to communicate with the board?

_____

_____

_____

3. What communication strategies were successful in the past? What strategies did not seem to meet their needs?

_____

_____

_____

4. What is the general availability of board members for communication during the work week?

_____

_____

_____

The template in Figure 2.1 is normally developed using information from a variety of sources and targets obtaining general information related to the board's communication needs. Figure 2.2 was designed to assist you as you consider the communication needs of individual board members.

Figure 2.2 Individual Board Member Communication Needs Template

This template has been designed with key questions you may want to ask your board members in relation to their communication needs.

1. What kinds of key information do you want to stay informed about in relation to the operation of the school district?

    _____

    _____

2. What is your preferred method for receiving this information?

    _____

    _____

3. What kinds of information would require me to contact you immediately? What kinds of information are you comfortable waiting to receive on a weekly basis?

    _____

    _____

4. How would you feel about administrative staff members contacting you instead of me in some cases? What is the district's history related to administrator/school board communication?

    _____

    _____

5. What thoughts/ideas do you have to help us achieve good two-way communication?

    _____

    _____

    What did you learn as a result of this interview and how can this information be used to design a good communication plan?

    _____

    _____

    _____

SUCCESSFUL COMMUNICATION: FORM AND FREQUENCY

Form and frequency related to board member communication varies by district and individual superintendent. The key is to develop an overall communication plan, but this is a step many superintendents do not embrace as they begin their new positions. As a new superintendent, you are on a sharp learning curve, expected to quickly understand the district's unique issues while at the same time meeting hoards of people, many wanting to bend your ear regarding an issue of political importance. New superintendents, in many cases, are overloaded by complicated demands and fail to take the time to develop a communication plan as described earlier. In the absence of a plan, many new superintendents randomly choose their communication strategy, often without establishing form or frequency.

Forms of Communication

Once communication needs are identified, it is important to hone in on the methods or forms to be used. In Table 2.1 we provide an outline of a few communication methods and include the pros, cons, and common strategies employed with each. As you review this figure, evaluate the methods based on your comfort level and the needs of your board members.

Typically superintendents choose to communicate with individual board members using one of the four primary methods listed in Table 2.1: e-mail, phone calls, hardcopy, or face-to-face meetings. Each has its advantages and disadvantages, but in combination these methods allow superintendents to successfully communicate with their boards.

A Special Note About E-Mail Communication

In this day and age of e-mail communication the process of equal contact with board members has become much easier, but in most states your e-mail is part of the public record and thus can be open to review. Additionally, you need to remember that sending an e-mail to board members should take place in stages. In essence, you need to make sure that less than a majority (a quorum) receives your e-mail at one time so that if they reply, a violation of your state's open meeting law does not occur.

In Table 2.2 we have included a list of communication ideas and items to consider which can be used by superintendents. We include this list to give you a jump-start in the communication process with your board.

Although this list of ideas is not meant to be all encompassing, it does provide an opportunity for you to begin thinking about the day-to-day intricacies of your communication with the board. Superintendent–board communication is distinct with each superintendent and each board. The forms of communication used will vary based upon the unique character of the institution and the individuals involved.

Table 2.1   Superintendent–Board Member Communication Methods

Methods	Pros	Cons	Strategies
E-Mail	• Easily produced • Efficient (in most cases takes less time than phone calls) • Preferred method by many individuals • Provides documentation of communication	• E-mail is part of public record • Some board members might see it as impersonal • Can be easily forwarded on to others (lacks confidentiality) • Limits opportunity for expanded conversation • Can violate open meeting laws if sent to all board members simultaneously	• Use as a method to communicate non-confidential information • Ask the school district's attorney for a confidentiality statement to place as a permanent footer on all outgoing e-mail messages • In initial individual meetings with each board member determine their preferred communication method • Can be used as periodic, scheduled communication strategy
Phone Call	• Provides quick feedback • Reasonably efficient • Offers personal touch to communication • Provides opportunity for expanded conversation • Allows for confidential conversation	• Require respondent's availability to establish communication • Not as efficient as e-mail, especially if multiple individuals are to be contacted • Hard to document content of conversation	• Establish preferred contact times with individuals and record for future use • Establish call log to confirm when conversations take place
Hard Copy	• Easily documented • Provides opportunity to include attachments without scanning • More formal than e-mail or phone communication	• Time consuming to develop and distribute • Reproduced easily (lacks confidentiality)	• Lends itself well to normal communication strategy (i.e., Friday update of the week's activities for the board) • Provide cover sheet with hardcopy communication indicating that some material may be confidential
Face-to-Face Meeting	• Most personal form of communication • Establishes rapport • Provides venue for expanded discussion • Provides greater opportunity to assess reaction to items being communicated	• Most inefficient method of communication, very time consuming • Can be difficult with detractors • Hard to document content of message	• Most effective when established as a communication method early in the superintendent's tenure • Best way to establish "equal time" standard, especially when meetings are conducted with each board member prior to board meeting to review agenda • In situations where important or difficult information is discussed, produce a summary of issues addressed and e-mail to individual as a way to document conversations • If, through expanded conversation, important issues are discussed or ideas generated, make sure to send an e-mail to other board members as a follow up to keep everyone in the loop

Table 2.2   Superintendent–Board Communication Ideas and Considerations

Communication Ideas	Items to Consider
E-Mail Options: • Send out weekly school district update via e-mail. • Employ an e-mail communication system which provides updates to board members (and others) when the district's Web site is modified. • Use e-mail as a means to communicate efficiently during periods of crisis. • Utilize e-mail to prompt thinking related to a topic of importance prior to a board workshop. • Apply e-mail as a method to distribute general school board communication in an efficient manner.	• Be careful not to ask board members to make decisions via e-mail, which could be construed as conducting a meeting without public notice. • Keep in mind that e-mail is public information.
Phone Call Options: • Use phone calls to add emphasis to an important message (such as the district receiving an award, or to discuss a lawsuit which is pending). • Call board members to simply "check in" and see how they are doing, or to ask whether they have questions regarding anything that is going on in the district. • Contact board members via phone when you need to discuss personnel issues. Use of e-mail in this situation is inappropriate. • Consider district-provided cell phones for board members to enhance communication (this options will have its pros and cons).	• Always use phone calls to add a personal touch, but because of their time consuming nature, apply this form of communication purposefully. • Set the standard early on in your superintendency that phone calls will be used as one form of communication, but not likely the predominate form (realizing that for certain board members it might be the predominate form if they are not technologically proficient).
Hard Copy Options: • Send out hard copy of items which you want to guard against being widely distributed (mark as confidential). • Send out thank you cards or birthday cards to board members to further build relationship. • Use hard copy to communicate all legal documents.	• Over time move board members away from hard copy communication as they are cumbersome and inefficient. • Analyze which items are appropriate for hard copy communication and design a migration process for other documents.

Face-to-Face Meeting Options:
• Establish early on in your superintendency a regular timeline to meet with each board member to discuss the following questions:
  ○ As a district are we aligning our operations with our vision, mission, and goals?
  ○ Are we effectively measuring our performance against our vision, mission, and goals?
  ○ What are things you are excited about in the district?
• Identify things that require attention in the district.
• Prior to attending school events prepare yourself by thinking about what the three most pressing issues are at that point in the district. This will prepare you for discussion that is likely to take place with board members and others at these events.
• Use face-to-face meetings to communicate the most confidential of information.
	• Identify other locally important issues to discuss during your face-to-face meetings with board members.
	• Always record in writing the outcome of face-to-face conversations with board members for future reference.

Frequency of Communication

Frequency of communication with board members can be broken down into two primary areas: emergency and normal communication. Emergency communication will take place periodically, but should follow the tenets of the communication plan that was discussed earlier. It is important to understand when communication should take place and surrounding which set of issues. Each board will see emergency communication in a different manner and thus this issue should never be taken for granted. As previously mentioned it is also important to understand the board president's role in the process of emergency communication.

With emergency communication, it is also crucial to understand how the superintendent can most efficiently and effectively make contact with individual board members. Some may want you to call their office, while others may not want any contact at their place of business. Certain board members may only be available via e-mail and others want to be contacted via cell phone. Regardless of the method, it is important to clearly understand how you will engage board members quickly and efficiently, especially in times of crisis.

Normal, ongoing communication is much more purposeful, but again should be borne out of the communication plan. It provides an opportunity to consider many different methods for planned, periodic communication, but as with emergency communication, should be a function of identified board member preferences. The goal of normal communication is much different than its counterpart in that it is aimed at providing information on an ongoing basis. Normal communication is very important to establish as it indicates your willingness to be open with the board. The board expects you to make normal communication a priority, but typically will be open regarding the methods you select. As stated earlier, the important issue is to develop a communication plan and dutifully stick to it.

Key Point #6: In the establishment of your communication plan, be sure to address communication forms and frequency.

ESTABLISHING EFFECTIVE SUPERINTENDENT–BOARD CHAIR/PRESIDENT COMMUNICATION

The superintendent-board chair/president relationship is unique and requires special attention. Below, in Figure 2.3, we have provided an interview template for you to use when establishing communication guidelines with your board chair/president.

Figure 2.3 Board Chair/President Interview Template

This template has been designed with the key questions you may want to ask your board chair/president in relation to his or her communication needs.

1. Due to the unique nature of your position as board chair/president, what kinds of key information do you want to stay informed about in relation to the operation of the school district?

    _____

    _____

2. How do you want to work together to develop the board meeting agenda?

    _____

    _____

3. What is your preferred method for receiving this information?

    _____

    _____

4. What kinds of information would require me to contact you immediately? How do you want to handle the notification of other board member related to this crucial information?

    _____

    _____

5. What thoughts/ideas do you have to help us achieve good two-way communication?

    _____

    _____

6. What did you learn as a result of this interview and how can the information be used to design a good communication plan?

    _____

    _____

EMERGENCY COMMUNICATION STANDARDS

From time to time, situations arise that require immediate communication and fast decisions. While these vary from district to district, the following list outlines some of the more common "emergencies" we have encountered in our work with superintendents that require immediate board contact:

- A bus accident
- A parent has gone to the media about a situation they are displeased about
- A fundraising drive has encountered a negative situation
- The death or severe illness of an employee
- The death or severe illness of a board member
- A board member has been arrested or accused of a crime
- An employee has been arrested or accused of a crime
- A former employee has been accused of a major crime
- A child has been abducted from a school
- An attempt has been made to abduct a child at a school
- An athletic team has been accused of a rules violation
- A water main has broken in one of the district buildings
- The heating system has failed in one of the district buildings
- School is being dismissed because of severe weather
- School is starting late because of severe weather
- A worker has been injured or killed while working on a district project
- Students have decided to protest at a local school
- Major vandalism has occurred in a district building

Most of these examples required that the superintendent immediately contact the school board. This contact is necessary so the board is well informed and not taken by surprise when members hear about the incident "out on the street." Develop minimum standards related to when you, as superintendent, should contact board members and, separately, the board chair/president (this is important because it could be different). Some boards may leave it to your discretion entirely, but we recommend working with your board to set some standards and procedures for emergency notification procedures. Figure 2.4 contains a template for your use in working with the board to design the parameters for emergency related communication.

Key Point #7: Be purposeful in designing a process related to when and how you will make contact with your board when emergency situations arise.

Figure 2.4 Emergency Communication Processes and Procedures

Use this form to plan the emergency communication parameters and procedures within your school district.

Situation	Board Contact Priority High = Immediate Medium = Within three hours Low = Next day	Preferred Contact Method (phone, face-to-face, e-mail, etc.)
1.		
2.		
3.		
4.		
5.		
6.		
7.		
8.		
9.		
10.		

MAINTENANCE OF YOUR
COMMUNICATION PLAN WITH THE BOARD

Even if you have put in the time to develop and implement a good communication plan, it is natural for issues and situations to arise that cause the plan to deteriorate. As circumstances and problems cause stress, as people become busy, as you and your board members begin to develop your own ideas, and as you naturally begin to talk with some members more than others, the chance for misunderstandings and a feeling of neglect can set in. This can be a critical time in the superintendent–board relationship and may require a "refocusing" or "refinement" of the original plan. In our work with superintendents and as we have served in the position, we have found that building in a barometer to gauge board member perceptions it vital. This information can be used to refocus or refine communication plans, which then have a much greater degree of success in maintaining positive relationships with board members. Those superintendents who do not regularly assess the perceptions of their board may not see the negative ideas held by some members. Disgruntled board members have been known to use their negative attitudes to build cases against their superintendents and ultimately turn the rest of the board members against them, similar to the situation faced by Ed at the beginning of this chapter.

> **Key Point #8:** Periodically review the impact of your communication plan with your board members. Make the necessary adjustments and refinements to your plan and your strategies to maintain good superintendent–board relations.

BOARD STANDARDS AND OPERATING PROTOCOLS

Once hired, smart superintendents typically go through an initial retreat process with their boards, in part to establish expectations, roles, and responsibilities. This is an important process as it provides everyone in the superintendent–board relationship the ability to get started on the right foot. Many new superintendents are afraid to engage in this process of setting expectations, as they don't want to address controversial topics early in their tenure. The problem is that if these items are not addressed early they are rarely discussed until a problem arises. One strategy to consider in addressing these topics is to ask either the search consultant who was engaged in your hiring process, or possibly someone from the state administrators' or school boards' association, to facilitate this retreat. In many cases an "independent" third party can raise issues and discuss topics that would be uncomfortable for the superintendent or board to broach alone. Use of a third party can also lend credibility to this important process, which allows everyone to feel like they are "doing the right thing" in addressing these critical questions.

One subset of this discussion is a review of the board's ethics standards, or development of a board operating protocol. Personally we prefer the establishment of an operating protocol for several reasons. Board ethics standards are typically part of adopted school district policy and, at a maximum, are perused annually as part of the board's self-evaluation process. The problem is that although these ethics standards are likely well written and contain important information, their use has become pedestrian. A board operating protocol, on the other hand, can be adopted, or reaffirmed, each successive year as part of the board's reorganization and used on an ongoing basis, which calls attention to its significant tenets. It can also be reworked on an annual basis as issues arise which require attention. The board may also want to establish an intervention system as part of its operating protocol for members who violate its tenets. Sanctions that range from a verbal warning by the board president to censure, can be considered as a way to bring a level of importance to the process.

In Figure 2.5 we have provided an example of components included in a board ethics policy that can be adapted through the retreat process to serve the unique needs of your district.

Figure 2.5 Sample Ethics Standards

Board Ethics Standards

- Attend all regularly scheduled board meetings insofar as possible, and become informed concerning the issues to be considered at those meetings.
- Recognize that decisions should be made only after discussion at publicly held board meetings.
- Render all decisions based on available facts and independent judgment, and refuse to surrender that judgment to individuals or special-interest groups.
- Encourage the free expression of opinion by all board members, and seek systematic communication between the board and students, staff, and all elements of the community.
- Work with other board members to establish effective board policies and to delegate authority for the administration of the schools to the superintendent.
- Communicate to other board members and the superintendent expressions of public reaction to board policies and school programs.
- Be informed about current educational issues by individual study and through participation in programs providing needed information, such as those sponsored by state and national school boards associations.

(Continued)

Figure 2.5 (Continued)

- Support the employment of persons best qualified to serve as school staff members, and insist on a regular and impartial evaluation of all personnel.

- Avoid being placed in a position of conflict of interest, and refrain from using board position for personal or partisan gain.

- Take no private action that will compromise the board or administration, and respect the confidentiality of information that is privileged under applicable law.

- Remember always that a board member's first and greatest concern must be the educational welfare of the students attending the public schools.

SOURCE: Found on the Arizona School Boards Association Web site at: http://lp.ctspublish.com/asba/public/lpext.dll?f=templates&fn=main-h.htm

Figure 2.6 Sample Board Operating Protocol

Achievement Valley Public School Board Operating Protocol

For the purpose of enhancing teamwork among members of the board and between the board and administration, we, the members of the Achievement Valley School Board, do hereby publicly commit ourselves collectively and individually to the following operating protocol:

- Surprises to the board or the superintendent will be the exception, not the rule. There should be no surprises at a board meeting. We agree to ask the board chair or the superintendent to place an item on the agenda instead of bringing it up unexpectedly at the meeting.

- Communication between staff and the board are encouraged. However, board requests that will likely require considerable time or have political implications are to be directed to the board chair and/or superintendent. All personnel complaints and criticisms received by the board or its individual members will be directed to the superintendent.

- The last stop, not the first, will be the school board. We agree to follow the chain of command and insist that others do so. While the board is eager to listen to its constituents and staff, each inquiry is to be referred to the person who can properly and expeditiously address the issue.

- As a parent, a board member retains the right to express his or her own personal opinions in verbal and/or written form.

- A board member will not "solicit an issue," become a "ball carrier" for others, or work around administrative employees and will encourage others to present their own issues, problems, or proposals in a constructive manner.

- The board will emphasize planning, policy making, and public relations rather than becoming involved in the management of the schools.

- The board will address its behavior by yearly self-evaluation and by addressing itself to any individual problems, such as poor meeting attendance or leaks of confidential information.

- The board will set clear goals for themselves and the superintendent. The board and superintendent will set clear goals for the Achievement Valley Public Schools.

- The superintendent is the chief executive officer and should recommend, propose, or suggest on most matters before the board.

- Individual board members do not have authority. Only the board as a whole has authority. We agree that an individual board member will not take unilateral action. The board chair will communicate the position(s) of the board on controversial issues.

- When board members serve on various school committees their role shall be defined by the board as silent observer or active participant.

- Conduct at a board meeting is very important. We agree to avoid words and actions that create a negative impression on an individual, the board, or the district. While we encourage debate and differing points of view, we will do it with care and respect to avoid an escalation of negative impressions or incidents. Individual members may disagree with a board action, but will support the decision of the board as a whole.

- To be efficient and effective, long board meetings must be avoided. Points are to be made in as few words as possible; speeches at board meetings will be minimal. If a board member believes he or she doesn't have enough information or has questions, either the superintendent or the board chair is to be called before the meeting.

- Board meetings are for decision making, action, and votes, not endless discussion.

- We agree to "move the question" when discussion is repetitive.

- The board will not play to the audience. We agree to speak to the issues on the agenda and attend to our fellow board members. Facts and information needed from the administration will be referred to the superintendent.

- The board will represent the needs and interests of all the children in the Achievement Valley Public Schools.

Board Chair

Board Member

Board Member

Board Member

Board Member

Date

WHO HAS AUTHORITY FOR WHAT: THE BOARD AND SUPERINTENDENT AS A TEAM

A question often asked by board members and superintendents is, "What is the role of the board versus the role of the superintendent in the operation of the school district?" The age-old statement that the board sets policy and the superintendent administers that policy would seem to indicate a very distinct and clear dividing line between the respective roles of each. That division, however, is not always so clear nor is it one upon which everyone involved agrees.

Board members are usually "doers"; they operate businesses, they run homes, they dig ditches, they buy supplies. "Doers" often find it hard to look at the big overall picture and make decisions that cause other people to "do" the job. Many times they are tempted to get in and "do" the job themselves. Conflict situations arise when the board and the superintendent have not defined their specific roles within the district.

Because the needs of a district vary, and because leadership and management styles are different, there are no universal answers to "who has the authority for what." The real need in each district is for the board and superintendent to decide what each is to do and establish proper procedures and policy that will lead to the performance of those duties.

Board members, as they make decisions and find themselves involved in the business of the district, should ask themselves: Are we providing leadership to the superintendent and staff and establishing policy for the district or have we stepped into the role of the administration? Superintendents should ask themselves: Am I providing leadership to the board in pointing out areas where policy is needed, or am I usurping the board's responsibility by establishing policy? Worse yet, am I forcing the board to make administrative decisions because I don't want to take responsibility?

Keeping roles clear and communication open is the key to good superintendent–board relations. In Table 2.3 a chart listing the possible division of roles and responsibilities between the board and superintendent is provided.

Consider the following tips regarding board standards and operating protocols:

- Superintendents either conduct a retreat or ask a third party to meet with the board early in their tenure to discuss expectations, roles, and responsibilities.
- Board standards, which are located in policy, are typically well written, but not reviewed with any frequency.
- Board operating protocols lend themselves to annual review, ongoing use and needed revision. Board member signatures should be included in an effective board operating protocol.

Table 2.3   Typical Roles/Responsibilities of the Board and Superintendent

Task	School Board Role/ Responsibility	Superintendent Role/ Responsibility
1. Policy	Adopts	Implements and suggests
2. Meetings	In charge of	Serves as a resource person
3. Budgets/Finance/ Audits	Adopts and monitors	Prepares, administers, monitors details
4. Instruction	Establish criteria, approves and monitors	Recommends, oversees staff's efforts
5. Personnel	Establishes criteria, approves or rejects	Interviews, recommends, hires, evaluates, promotes staff development
6. Facilities/ Transportation/ Food Services	Develops policy on use of facilities, transportation, food services	Implements policy, writes rules and regulations, makes recommendations
7. Community Relations	Creates a positive image for district	Creates a positive image for district, directs communication
8. The Board and Superintendent	Hires the superintendent, establishes expectations, evaluates	Works at the pleasure of the board, is chief executive officer of the district

SOURCE: Adapted from the Nebraska Association of School Boards.

- Board operating protocols are most effective when they include board member designed interventions for violations of the protocol.

SUMMARY

In Chapter 2 we have examined the crucial relationship between the superintendent and the board. This relationship is one of the most important to your career and ultimately the stability and success of the school district. As you prepare to start working on the ideas and strategies you feel will help establish and maintain a good relationship with your board, think about the following questions that highlight the information presented in this chapter:

- How can you determine the board's culture related to the super-intendent–board relationship?
- How will you address the necessary aspects of communicating with your board?
- Why is it important to define the role of the board chair/president and get the entire board to agree on your unique relationship with this person?
- Why are board operating protocols an important part of your superintendency?
- How can you treat each board member equally and meet their unique needs?
- At what point will you develop a superintendent–board communication plan?

Having a good relationship with your board members is not impossible, but it does take work on both your part and theirs. Superintendents who nurture this relationship tend to have stability in their district and are able to work through issues in a positive and productive manner. Those who don't put much time in building relationships with their board members or see it as a burden could be headed for trouble. We hope you have discovered some good ideas in this chapter that will help you as you work to build positive relationships with your board members.

In Chapter 3, Organizational Trust and Culture: What Every Superintendent Should Know, we move beyond building a relationship with your board and focus on ideas to help you work with your staff and the community. From our experiences, those superintendents that are able to develop trusting relationships with their staff are headed for success and smooth operations; those who try to move forward without these key components run into land mines on a consistent basis.

3

Organizational Trust and Culture

What Every Superintendent Should Know

Being taken for granted can be a compliment. It means that you've become a comfortable, trusted person in another person's life.

—Joyce Brothers

Bonnie, a new superintendent, was organized and ready to go. She had talked with board members and performed her own independent assessment of what needed to be done in the district. Since she was always a "mover and shaker" as a principal, she knew that she had to get right to work. Bonnie was going to implement a new plan for improving the teaching and learning in the district.

After only a short time in the new program, she began to see resistance in the teachers and principals in the district. When asked about the problem, several of the staff members were very general in their responses to her. They told her that things would get better. One or two of Bonnie's closest confidants told her that she had not yet developed trusting relationships with the staff. People were still checking her out to see if she meant what she had said. They were holding off on the project until they could see if they could trust Bonnie. She had to work hard to build relationships with the staff members before the project could go on.

In this example, Bonnie learned an important lesson related to her work as a superintendent; the importance of trust. Luckily for her, several of her administrators felt comfortable enough with her to tell her why she was facing problems with her new implementation plan. Many new superintendents are not so lucky!

ABOUT THIS CHAPTER

Trust and the confidence of others is a key aspect of effective leadership. Without trust leaders cannot lead. In this chapter we will discuss ways to naturally develop trust as you begin to work in your school district. As you read the chapter, pay attention to the following points:

- Understanding and diagnosing your district's culture
- How rapport, trust, and climate relate to your district's culture
- Considering the importance of trust in the organization
- Methods for building and sustaining trust in the organization
- The power of the organization's culture as a gatekeeper of excellence
- Working with employee groups to build excellence and trust

ORGANIZATIONAL CULTURE

School districts can be complex and diverse in their very nature. As a new superintendent, you will need to understand the culture of the organization. This important aspect of a school district will give you clues to how things have operated in the past, what kinds of norms are in place, how people may react to your new questions and ideas, and a variety of other information you will find crucial to your success.

While many authors talk about culture, Edgar Schein has written much on the topic. We selected his work to highlight in this chapter because many other works on this topic are grounded by the principles he pioneered. In his book, *Organizational Culture and Leadership* (1997), Schein provides the following thoughts:

> The culture of a group . . . can be defined as a pattern of shared basic assumptions that the group learned as it solved its problems of external adaptation and internal integration, that has worked

well enough to be considered valid and, therefore, to be taught to new members as the correct way to perceive, think, and feel in relation to those problems. (Schein, 1997, p. 12)

Schein provides a listing of the most common attributes that are shared by groups. We have provided this list below to help you understand the present culture of your school district.

1. Observed behavioral regularities when people interact (the language they use, the rituals in place, etc.)
2. Group norms (the implicit standards and values that evolve)
3. Espoused values (the articulated and public principles and values the group appears to be seeking to achieve)
4. Formal philosophy (the broad policies that guide the group's actions toward stakeholders)
5. Rules of the game (the implicit rules for getting along in the organization)
6. Climate (the feeling that is conveyed by the group related to physical layout, interactions, etc.)
7. Embedded skills (the special competencies group members display in accomplishing certain tasks)
8. Habits of thinking/mental models (the shared cognitive frame or "ways of thinking" used by members)
9. Shared meanings (emergent understandings shared by group members)
10. Root metaphors or integrating symbols (the ideas, feelings, and images developed by the group to characterize itself). (Schein, 1997, pp. 8–10)

These attributes work together to define the culture of any organization. As a new superintendent it will be important for you to find a way to assess the district's culture and see how you fit into it. The template in Table 3.1 will assist you as you begin this task.

Even though it may seem like a complex task to undertake as you are also working hard to get to know the school district and all of the players in that arena, we believe keeping a notebook where you can jot down some ideas related to organizational culture will be fruitful for you. As you get to know "how things are done around here," you will begin to see how you can move forward to make needed changes while still respecting certain aspects of the organization's culture.

We also recommend that you ask your cabinet or administrative team to complete the District Culture Diagnosis Template. Typically these individuals have served in the district for some time and their insights can be quite helpful to you as well.

Table 3.1   District Culture Diagnosis Template

District Cultural Aspect	Evidence Gathered (through observations, interviews, reviewing artifacts, etc.)	Description of Culture Related to Evidence (What is the culture like in this area?)
Observed behavioral regularities: What kinds of language do people use; how do they interact in formal and informal settings?		
Group norms: What kinds of formal and informal rules seem to govern meetings and work relationships?		
Espoused values: What kinds of values does the group use in achieving its goals; what are the group's goals and aspirations?		
Formal philosophy: How does the group view and treat stakeholders?		
Rules of the game: What does it take to get along here and be successful?		
Climate: What is the physical layout of the work environments; what is the feel of the organization?		
Embedded skills: What special skills are required/developed to be successful in this environment?		
Habits of thinking/mental models: How do people process and problem-solve here; what assumptions guide their thinking?		
Shared meanings: What informal language or slang exists here; what inside information do people need to know in order to "get it."		
Root metaphors or integrating symbols: What images or icons seem to describe the group or help them relate in their work here?		

Key Point #1: Take time to get to know the culture of your district. Culture can be difficult to change quickly, so be sure you have a thorough understanding of its nuances prior to moving forward.

RAPPORT, TRUST, CLIMATE, AND THEIR RELATION TO CULTURE

Rapport, trust, and climate are crucial aspects to the success of an organization and its leader, and are directly related to your success in entering the new culture. These are elements that you need to think about in helping to build a successful school organization as its new chief executive. In this section, we will talk briefly about these elements and their significance to your success as a new superintendent.

Rapport: Rapport is a term that relates to the interpersonal relationship between two parties on a moment-to-moment basis. Since rapport is based on moment-to-moment interactions, the strategies that help to build rapport tend to be interpersonal in nature, such as looking at another person while you are speaking to him or her, sincerely smiling when something interests you, giving personal regard to another, and so on.

Trust: Trust relates to a group's understanding that both the group itself and the individuals within the group are reliable (Tarter, as reported in Kochanek, 2005, p. 7). Trust is built on the summation of many experiences with a person. The elements of integrity, reliability, honesty, competence, and personal regard work together to help you develop a sense of trust with another person.

Climate: Climate is an aspect that relates to the day-to-day tone or feeling in the organization. As the chief executive officer of a school district you help to set the climate of the organization through your words and actions. Climate is important because it leads to the establishment of the culture of the organization.

The elements of rapport, trust, and climate can be vehicles that you have an impact on as the superintendent. While you may not be able to impact the culture in the short-term, you can build rapport, develop trusting relationship, and implement strategies to nurture a positive district climate. Let's look at some of the elements we just introduced in more detail.

THE IMPORTANCE OF TRUST

In Chapter 1, we talked about the high level of visibility you will experience as a superintendent. Since you are so visible, the concepts of rapport, trust, climate, and culture are very important to your success. You will be more visible than most of your counterparts in other businesses and organizations in your community.

In the groundbreaking book, *The Leadership Challenge*, Kouzes and Posner (2007) discuss many principles essential to excellent leadership performance. We selected to discuss this book because of the long-term nature of the work and the fact that the authors have been gathering research regarding their assertions for a number of years. The book is currently in its fourth printing, first available on the market in 1987. It is unique in its content because most of the principles outlined in it are based on research. Since 1987, the authors have been asking people to respond to a survey outlining important characteristics of leaders. Over the past 25 years, the following four leadership attributes have been rated the highest:

- Honesty
- Forward Thinking
- Inspiring
- Competent (Kouzes & Posner, 2007, p. 29)

Here are some general thoughts about how these elements may impact you as the new superintendent of a school district.

Honesty: As the superintendent, people will look to you for honesty. They may be evaluating your words and promises during your first few months in office. People may not like bad news but they expect you to tell the truth and be straightforward. Be careful in what you promise people. You may not remember what you promised, but others will. Keep the importance of honesty in mind as you assume your new position.

Forward Thinking: People will be looking for you to help them dream and imagine their future within the parameters of the existing culture. As a new leader, they will expect you to be thinking about how to keep the organization moving forward.

Inspiring: Good leaders know how to make people feel good about themselves and excited about their work in the district. You can inspire people through your actions and words. Some superintendents forget about the inspirational part of their job, but this can be a good way for you to connect with and become a part of the district culture.

Competent: Competence relates to your ability to build confidence in others. You build the feeling of competence through focusing on doing your job, making accurate statements, and acting with integrity. Competence is something you build over time within your school district.

Key Point #2: Remember that trust is an important commodity for you to possess as a superintendent. The amount a trust you have may depend on your ability to connect and build confidence with others.

BUILDING AND SUSTAINING ORGANIZATIONAL TRUST

While there are many authors who write on the topic of trust, we have chosen a few that provide education-related ideas. A recent book titled *Building Trust for Better Schools* (Kochanek, 2005) outlines some of the work that is being done in this area. Trust is so important to effective school operations that author Julie Reed Kochanek reports this finding in an early part of the book:

> The latest research on trust in schools has even demonstrated a positive relationship between trust and school effectiveness, making a connection between the growth of trust and organizational changes, which can lead to improved educational outcomes for students. (Bryk & Schneider, 2002; Gooddard, Tschannen-Moran, & Hoy, 2001; Hoy, Tarter & Witkoskie, 1992; as reported in Kochanek, 2005, p. 6)

Building trust may not only be the tool a new superintendent uses to help implement new ideas and initiatives, but its presence in a school may also positively impact student learning. Margaret Wheatley, in her book *Leadership and the New Science* (1995), contends that values and behaviors have a way of permeating through organizations. If a value or behavior appears in one part of the organization, it will show up somewhere else even if the two parts of the organization are in limited contact. The trust you build and value as a superintendent has a way of trickling down to other parts of the organization. Since trust is an important part of increasing student achievement, you help impact student achievement through your efforts to build trust.

Kochanek defines trust in schools by adding:

> The body of work coming out of [The] Ohio State University from Hoy and his colleagues (Tarter et al., 1989, p. 295) defines trust as a group understanding that both the group itself and the individuals within the group are reliable. Further conceptual study from this group led to a description of the five components of faculty trust: benevolence, reliability, competence, honesty, and openness. (Hoy & Tschannen-Moran, 1999; as reported in Kochanek, pp. 6–7)

If these are the components that faculty see as helping build trust within their own particular group, they are also good for you to keep in mind as you work to build trust with your faculty. In organizations outside of schools and school districts, people develop trust by communicating their expectations for each other in an outward fashion. Kochanek (p. 7) contends that in schools there is less open communication about roles so people are forced to use indirect methods to assess other people's expectations of role fulfillment.

This impacts you as a new superintendent because there may not be much formal communication about your role and the expectations for you to fulfill your role. People in the district may be building (or not building) their relationships with you based on assumptions rather than facts. Take whatever opportunities you can to open up dialog about your role and their expectations. This will help ensure that you are working to build trust.

Key Point #3: Since many people will be judging you based on their expectations rather than reality, try to open up communication about their expectations whenever possible. This behavior will go a long way in helping you meet expectations and build trust within your school community.

Later in her book, Kochanek outlines ideas for school leaders to use in building trust. Possible strategies to build trust in general include the following:

- Develop open communication about roles and expectations.
- Be clear in defining work expectations (work "contracts").
- Show integrity by sharing your beliefs related to what is best for children, then following through on those beliefs.
- Use personal regard when dealing with others.
- Provide familiarity with diverse groups (socially, ethnically, etc.) by providing opportunities to communicate and interact through social exchanges.
- Lower the perception of venerability that some groups may feel in interactions.
- Engage in simple activities to build a base for more complex activities later.
- Follow through on what you promise; avoid overpromising. (adapted from Kochanek, 2005, pp. 7–32)

Examples of simple activities that can help build trust in groups are contained in the Figures 3.1 and 3.2.

Figure 3.1   Defining Group Operating Norms

Understanding the expectations of the group you are working with is an important part of your success as a first-year superintendent. In smaller school districts
you may interact with almost every constituent on a regular basis, while in larger
districts you may only directly interact with a small number of people. Use this
exercise with the group(s) that you feel would be most appropriate.

1. Divide your group up into smaller teams of 5–6 people on each team.

2. Provide each group with chart paper and several markers.

3. Ask one member of each group to be the scribe and write down the results
    from the conversation in the group.

4. Pose the following questions to the group:

    • What are your expectations for me as your superintendent?

    • What are your expectations of the organization?

    • What are your expectations of you, as a member of this organization?

5. Have each scribe write down the results from the group's discussion of the
    questions.

6. Ask each group to present the results of their discussion using the chart.

7. Collect all of the charts, compile the results, and share them with the group
    at a future meeting. Be sure to share the expectations that you can honor and
    those that may be difficult or impossible for you to meet. Have a group dialog
    about these and their impact on the school district.

8. Compile the results of this discussion. Have the information formatted in a
    way that will help you remember the expectations so you will be able to
    honor them as you move forward. Some superintendents have the expecta-
    tions reproduced on note cards while others place them in their office as a
    reminder of their commitment.

Key Point #4: In order to build a trusting atmosphere you will need
to conduct some activities that let people get to know you and allow
you to understand their expectations for you in your role as their
superintendent.

Figure 3.2 Artifact Introductions

This activity is designed to help a group get to know a lot about each other in a short period of time. It also helps a group to build deep and meaningful relationships that will be key to the operation of the organization.

Here is how it works:

1. Ask participants to bring an item or artifact to the first meeting of a group that represents them either personally or professionally. Let them know they will have an opportunity to take one minute to share their artifact and how it represents them with the entire group.

2. At the first meeting of the group, remind individuals of the parameters of the activity; each person will share their artifact for one to two minutes and talk about how the artifact describes him or her in a personal or professional manner.

3. Be sure they understand the purpose of doing the activity: to get to know each other in a deeper manner so they can help each other in the future.

4. Have the entire group sit in a circle facing each other. As the leader/facilitator share your artifact first modeling the process for others.

5. For a group consisting of approximately twenty members, the activity usually lasts about forty minutes. For larger groups the activity may last over an hour. In these larger groups is a good idea to hold the artifact sharing over two separate sessions.

6. About halfway through a session it is a good idea to stop the activity, allow people a chance to stand and stretch, then have them talk with a partner about what they're learning about each other as result of the activity. Once the activity has been completed, be sure to debrief it by asking the groups to talk about what they have learned as a result of hearing other people's artifact introductions.

SOURCE: From Eller & Eller, (2008), *101 Strategies for Developing a Positive School Culture.*

ORGANIZATIONAL CULTURE: THE GATEKEEPER OF EXCELLENCE

The term gatekeeper conjures up various images in our minds depending upon our background and experience. Most of us think about an individual or organizational obstacle that plays the role of controlling what is acceptable. School districts, which are examples of the classic bureaucratic structure, tend to institute many such control points, some formal (policies, procedures, and so on) and others informal (organizational culture, hidden communication networks, and so on). Formal structures are similar across school districts and are typically designed in reaction to a perceived organizational need. Informal structures, such as an organization's culture, are much more complex and unwieldy. They are informal because no one initially sought to engineer their design or development; they just evolved over time based upon individuals in the organization and their personal characteristics. The challenge is that to be successful in implementing change processes or a new initiative, superintendents must understand the importance of organizational culture. It is our belief that a healthy, highly performing culture is a precursor to success in any school district or effective organization.

Properties of School Districts as Organizations

Bolman and Deal (1997), in their highly regarded book *Reframing Organizations: Artistry, Choice, and Leadership*, speak of properties that are found in organizations. These properties help to explain the complexity of human interaction that takes place in your school district and provides an opportunity for greater cultural insight. We have used this list of properties to highlight the challenges faced in school districts. Clearly school district cultures vary and function on a continuum. As Schwartz described (in Bolman & Deal, 1997), organizations are as likely to be snake pits as rose gardens.

Four properties identified by Bolman and Deal (1997) are listed below for consideration. They believe organizations are complex, surprising, deceptive, and ambiguous; we have added a fifth—that organizations exhibit characteristics of living organisms.

The Complexity of Organizations

Bolman and Deal (1997) point out that organizations are "populated by humans" and as such they can be very hard to understand. Human behavior is unpredictable at best and tends to be reactive to stimuli provided in any given situation.

School districts draw their complexity from the fact that they serve, as discussed in Chapter 1, numerous constituencies. Students, parents, teachers, classified staff, administrators, school board members, legislators (local, state, and federal), and community members all have a stake in your school system. Unfortunately they don't all see eye-to-eye regarding what the goals of the district should be. They all want to see the district deliver "quality education," but how is this defined? What does it look like at the school and district levels? Herein lays the problem. When you distill it down it can be very difficult, if not impossible, to get everyone on the same page. Each group wants to lobby for their individual interest in a structure that is constrained by a scarcity funding model. It takes a politically competent superintendent to keep the district on an even keel in this type of environment.

Organizations Are Surprising

How often have we developed an initiative which sounds great, and is designed to help students or staff in significant ways, but ends up failing for reasons which are not clearly understood? We recently observed a situation where a school district designed a hiring incentive program that was aimed at attracting teachers for very hard to fill positions. The program was developed, implemented, and sailed quite smoothly until more experienced members of the teaching staff took issue with the fact the district was focused on new hires, not retaining those who had been in the district. Although both issues were important, clearly the attempt to take care of one concern resulted in exacerbating the other. The district had to rethink its strategy and work toward designing a system that served everyone's needs. This is not at all uncommon, but is indicative of the types of surprises that are faced on a daily basis.

One explanation for why human organizations are full of surprises was provided by March and Olsen (1979) in their widely accepted Garbage Can Model of Organizational Choice. Although decades old, this theory continues to provide helpful insight into why we are oftentimes "surprised" by what takes place day to day in the school districts we serve. A garbage can is used as a metaphor to describe a place where many different ideas, thoughts, and concepts from various constituencies come together in a confined environment (the school district). Once in the garbage can these ideas, thoughts, and concepts are mixed together and often combine with other issues to form solutions. The process of this milieu being mixed together and the solutions that result help explain why outcomes tend to be so unpredictable. We simply cannot understand what will enter into the mix that day, or how issues might combine. It is because of this reality that we are truly at the mercy of human nature. We need to clearly understand that although we can anticipate outcomes on occasion, surprises will always be part of the mix in human organizations.

Organizations Are Deceptive

Bolman and Deal (1997) describe how a senior official in a large government agency indicated, "Communications in organizations are rarely candid, open, or timely." Although we would naively hope that this is not true in school districts, clearly it is, at least in concept. It is important to remember that school districts, like other bureaucracies, seek to remain stable at all cost. Status quo is what the organization desires, as any form of change is seen as a threat to its uniquely developed culture.

A key example of this "deception" relates to how some school districts, or other government entities, "cover up" their mistakes in an effort to forego public scrutiny. No one wants to be embarrassed, nor do they want to look "incompetent," thus extensive energy will at times be spent to protect the current state. We believe the word "deceptive" is too strong for most school district errors. A better word to describe this concept in school districts might be "transparency." Oftentimes school districts will not fully disclose the intricacies of a particular financial situation, as they do not want to face community or staff scrutiny. As an example, it may be that if the public is especially critical of the district's administrative costs, it will do what it can to code these costs to other areas of the budget so that the amount shown as "administrative" is decreased and looks better when compared to other districts in the area.

> **Key Point #5:** Keep in mind that your school district is made up of people and that people can be unpredictable and emotional. Don't underestimate the power of emotions in an organization. Responding appropriately can help enhance your sense of trust in the district.

Organizations Are Like Organisms

Although possibly a new paradigm for some educators, we submit that an organization's culture should be considered a living organism (Wheatley, 1995). Through maintaining the school district's beliefs, values, rituals, and history, its culture controls much of what takes place in the organization. This is especially important when considering the impact of change or new ideas in the organization. As a bureaucracy that seeks to maintain equilibrium (Hanson, 1998), school districts will most often treat new initiatives, or change processes, as a virus. As an example, a new initiative is proposed by the administration and, perceiving a change in the status quo, the organization's immune system (those individuals with the most to lose) seeks to thwart the new concept like a virus. If it succeeds, the organization foregoes the impact of disequilibrium and change and maintains its current state. On the other hand, if the new idea gains a foothold then the organization mounts an effort to fight back (Pritchett, 2002). This fight will typically be quite ugly and leaves many hard feelings for all involved. As such, this is the primary reason why superintendents must be knowledgeable regarding how the culture works in their district. Armed with a clear understanding of how cultures react to change, superintendents can prepare initiatives that are designed for success.

> What is critical is the relationship created between two or more elements. Systems influence individuals, and individuals call forth systems. It is the relationship that evokes the present reality. Which potential becomes real depends on the people, the events, and the moment. (Wheatley, 2005)

The "organization as an organism" concept tells us that, like a living thing, our organizations are made up of many integrated parts; when we impact one part of the organization, the other parts are also impacted. This is important to keep in mind as you move forward with changes and new ideas.

TRUST AND EXCELLENCE IN EMPLOYEE GROUP/UNION RELATIONSHIPS

One of the first things superintendents need to do when entering a new position is to establish themselves as the district's leader, while at the same time developing effective working relationships with employee groups/ unions. This is always a tough balancing act that takes a great deal of finesse to achieve. Invariably some employee groups/unions will agree with your vision and tough decisions; others won't. You need to realize there is a fine line between pandering for acceptance and establishing healthy relationships that can be sustained over time. It has been said that serving as superintendent of a school district is as close to being in an elected position as possible. We believe this to be true and therefore, to achieve success, superintendents develop a sixth sense related to dealing with people and working in a politically charged environment.

Unfortunately strong relationships with employee groups/unions are oftentimes the exception rather than the rule. Superintendent turnover continues to hover at all time highs and, in this age of strong accountability and scrutiny, this is likely not to change in the near future. The question is, how is trust and excellence achieved in employee group/union relationships? The answer to this question is at the heart of gaining support for change in your district. At best, implementing reform in school districts is difficult, but as many seasoned superintendents will tell you, it is impossible without active employee support.

> **Key Point #6:** The union/association relationship is important for you as the superintendent. Pay close attention to these relationships so you don't have any major employee group working behind your back to undermine you in your new role.

In Table 3.2 we identify traits and tactics that many superintendents use to establish effective employee group/union relationships.

To establish trust and excellence in employee group/union relationships each of the four traits or tactics listed in Table 3.2 must be implemented. Ongoing discussions should take place with employee groups/ unions to establish a culture of open communication and transparency.

In discussing the matter of employee group/union relationships we hope to provide a perspective that shows both trust and excellence can be

Table 3.2   Effective Employee Group/Union Relationship Traits and Tactics

Trait or Tactic	Description	Desired Outcome	Pitfalls
Actions = Respect	It is all about what you do, not what you say. This is one of the most difficult, yet rarely followed, tenets in establishing effective employee group/union relationships.	Trusting relationship with employee groups/unions.	Making a mistake in thinking employee groups/unions will be convinced with words.
Regular, Ongoing Meetings (at least monthly)	Meeting with employee groups/unions on a regular basis.	To establish relationship and a venue for open communication and problem solving.	Believing because these meetings are friendly that employee groups/unions will accept your initiatives.
Listening	People know whether you are listening to them, or if you are simply "doing your duty."	To show employee groups/unions that you truly want to listen and to understand.	Equating hearing someone with "listening" to them. In other words, people know when you are truly focused on them individually.
Honesty	To be open when trouble occurs or information is shared.	Employees trust what you say. This pays big dividends when problems occur.	Making the assumption that people will always trust you when attempting to take appropriate action. In some union relationships you will never be trusted.

achieved on some level in all school districts. This being said, we also are not naïve enough to believe it is possible in every context. In certain situations there is history that prevents a superintendent from achieving trust and excellence. The silver lining in these situations is that typically the animus is held by only a few, and if their influence can be overcome in one way, shape, or form, great strides can be realized.

Consider the following tips regarding effective employee group/union relationships:

- Remember that it is not what you say, but what you do which counts. Employee groups/unions will watch how you deal with situations and seek to establish a match between what you do and what you say. If you say one thing and do another, your credibility will be lost and it can be very difficult, if not impossible, to reestablish.

- Be cognizant of the fact that trust with employee groups/unions is difficult to establish, yet very easy to destroy.
- Listening skills are paramount to your success as a superintendent. Know how to listen in an engaged manner.

SUMMARY

Even though trust is a fundamental aspect of building positive relationships, the concept is elusive to many people. Since in your role as the superintendent almost one hundred percent of the work you do is with people, being able to build trust is a crucial part of your success. Over the years many authors have written about the importance of trust and how to build it with others, but it will be up to you to move the ball forward and make a real difference in your school district.

As you review the major concepts from this chapter, take a minute to reflect on the following questions:

- Why is trust so important to my success as a superintendent?
- What relationships exist between trust and school effectiveness?
- What processes do people go through in developing trusting relationships? How do people manage these processes?
- How do successful superintendents manage their relationships with unions and employee groups? What key elements seem to make the most sense when working with these groups?

Remember, trust is earned over time. Keep honesty and integrity at the forefront of your professional practice. Guard these elements carefully because once you have lost them, it a very difficult to get them back.

In Chapter 4, School Finance 101: What Should the Superintendent Know?, you will learn about another important area of effective leadership: budget management. In today's complex and scarce budget environment, good skills and understanding in this essential area has helped many superintendents be successful. The information in this chapter will give you a great start as you assume the superintendency.

4

School Finance 101

What Should the Superintendent Know?

The pure and simple truth is rarely pure and never simple.
—Oscar Wilde

A colleague we once worked with summed up superintendent operational success in three words: beans, buses, and business. "Beans" refers to the lunch program, "buses" refers to the transportation program, and "business" refers to the management of the school district budget.

We have seen in the previous chapters of this book that the modern day superintendency is much more complex than the assessment offered by our colleague, but the successful management of the school district budget is still a key area for success for you as superintendent. A perplexing question for new superintendents is, how much should I know about my district's finances? Chances are that you "came up through the ranks," first as a principal and possibly a central office administrator before your superintendency. You understood your building or department budget, but the school district budget is much more complex.

Can you simply rely upon the district's business manager to oversee the budget? Did you receive enough background knowledge through your school finance class to be successful? Since you are responsible for every aspect of the school district's budget, how can you quickly "get up to speed" and keep the district out of financial trouble?

ABOUT THIS CHAPTER

This chapter has been designed to help address the budgetary issues you will face as you start your superintendency. Since a school district's budget is very complex and the budgeting process varies from state to state, the information contained in this chapter is somewhat general in nature; we recommend connecting with state superintendents' organizations, other successful superintendents in your region, your own business manager, your state department of education, and other informed sources for the specialized information and guidance you may need to become a master at your state budgeting process.

In the spirit of providing you with the foundational information you will need to get started in understanding the budgeting process, the following major topics are outlined in this chapter:

- Obtaining key financial reports and deciphering their meaning
- The importance of long-range financial planning to the district's future
- Knowing what to ask about the school district's audit

STAYING AFLOAT: FOUR KEY FINANCIAL REPORTS

Can it be as easy as reviewing four monthly reports to keep your finger on the pulse of the district's financial situation? The colleagues we have worked with over the years have found the answer to be "yes!" A problem commonly faced by new superintendents is that they are not aware how to begin this process, thus they "blindly" rely on those charged with its responsibility. As you can imagine, this practice is very dangerous. These superintendents sit in meetings only understanding a portion of the conversation, hoping the ship won't hit a financial iceberg during their tenure. The greater travesty is there simply is not a good resource for superintendents to get a handle on the complexity of their district's finances. Superintendents are pulled in many different directions and they do not have the time to become financial experts, yet it is imperative they put in place the management tools to understand where the ship is headed.

> **Key Point #1:** Don't just rely on the expertise of your business manager to keep you informed about the district's financial status; find ways to quickly learn how to assess the financial health of the school district.

From our experience and the experiences of our colleagues, there are four key financial reports that can assist superintendents in their quest to understand the district's financial health and monitor its progress.

Key school district financial reports to monitor are:

- Enrollment Reports
- Expenditure Reports
- Revenue Reports
- Staffing Plans or Position Control Systems

Enrollment Reports

One principle all superintendents need to have a firm grasp on is the fact that enrollment drives funding. Although this is understood on a rudimentary level, what superintendents often do not think through is the fact that they can use current and previous year data to track enrollment trends and make projections. There are two primary reports superintendents should obtain from their finance staff (or the department charged with this function) to assess this area: the monthly enrollment report and the annual enrollment projection.

Monthly Enrollment Reports

As indicated above, the monthly enrollment report will originate in different locations depending upon the district's organizational structure, but the data and format should be consistent. The four primary components that should be present in a monthly enrollment report are the following:

- The current month's enrollment figures
- The previous year's enrollment at the same point in time as the current figure
- A statistical projection of what the district's enrollment was anticipated to be for the current month
- The enrollment figure which was used to build the current year's budget

The monthly enrollment report needs to tie back to the same figures that the state uses to deliver funding. In some states this may require additional thought during the development stage of the report. For example, the state of Minnesota funds schools based upon a function of Average Daily Membership (ADM), which is different than the daily headcount that may be used in the monthly enrollment report. The reason for mentioning this fact is to point out that it is important, especially in larger districts, to involve both your enrollment and finance staff in the design and development of the monthly enrollment report. States maintain different enrollment procedures and thus a collaborative effort will enable you to ensure your report is designed to provide accurate data.

Key Point #2: Work with your district's finance and/or enrollment staff to generate enrollment reports that clearly tie to school funding based on how your particular state determines this funding. If you don't, you may be basing your budget assumptions on "head count" rather than figures that translate to your school district's income. A disaster could result from this miscalculation.

A second yet equally important part of correlating enrollment figures to funding relates to comparing monthly enrollment to the district's budgeted enrollment, as mentioned above. As a component of the report, the superintendent should be able to see what the district's enrollment is for a particular month and then compare it to the number upon which the budget was built. Does current enrollment exceed this figure, or is there a decrease? These data provide you the opportunity to speak with district finance staff to determine how enrollment and ultimately the budget are progressing for the year. It may be that you are generating additional dollars in the current school year than was anticipated or spending more than you are taking in and will need to make modifications to the budget so the district's reserves are not hit too hard.

Insights gained from the data provided in your report will be considerably richer if current year information is compared to the same point in the previous year. This provides you the ability to see enrollment trends in the district, which can be very helpful in the decision making process. It is not at all uncommon that the student enrollment of a district might be large in the fall, but as a result of attrition, mobility, or other factors, starts to shrink in December. Understanding your district's unique trends enables you to achieve a better view regarding what might be happening with enrollment during certain parts of the school year.

Key Point #3: Keep an eye on enrollment trends in the current school year and tie them back to the historical trends that your district has gathered. This correlation will help you as you work with your board and staff in making decisions related to the budget.

It is also of tremendous importance to be able to predict what might be happening with your enrollment during the current year. This knowledge enables you to determine whether additional resources can be added, or reductions are required. Superintendents can use historical enrollment data to create a "crystal ball" of sorts, which enables them to "predict" where the district may be headed during that particular year. How this transpires is that the report needs to include a line that applies historical monthly trends to the months to come in the fiscal year. In other words, if you know the district's enrollment in the month of January was 5,000 and historical data indicate a typical decline of 1 percent between January and February, then you can "predict" February enrollment will be 4,950. This ability to "predict" where the district is headed during that particular fiscal year can be extremely helpful in the decision making process.

It should also be noted that in some states, like Arizona, a static figure is used to drive funding for the upcoming year. In Arizona that figure happens to be the hundreth day of the school year. Whatever your enrollment is on the hundreth day is how you will be funded during the next year. In addition, districts that are growing receive "growth funds" and those that are declining are reduced. The reason for mentioning this is that each state looks at enrollment from a different perspective, thus these nuances must be considered as you design your monthly enrollment report.

Another consideration relates to districts that are experiencing tremendous growth or decline. Both of these situations can create a real challenge when it comes to predicting the district's enrollment picture. Although we discuss the concept of annual enrollment projections below it must be noted that in these situations your budgeting processes must take on a very conservative approach. Many superintendents have faced situations where they approved a budget which assumed rapid growth only to be faced with cut backs when the district's predictions didn't materialize. Many will push you to hire staff to "prepare for growth," but it is a much safer approach to hire conservatively and then add staff as students show up. As educators we know this is not the preferred approach because we may be faced with hiring inferior staff late in the season, but it is fiscally prudent.

Key Point #4: Be conservative in your hiring practices, especially in situations where it appears the school district is experiencing rapid growth. The growth could disappear and your budget could be negatively impacted by the fact that you now have people on staff that you must pay for out of reserves or even borrowed money because the enrollment is not supporting their positions.

Districts facing enrollment decline experience a similar but much more challenging situation. In most circumstances declining enrollment is an equally difficult trend to assess, but is typically more taxing as it requires budget cuts. In some cases it is the result of a large business relocating its operations to another area, but in other circumstances it may be a slow movement of people out of the area. Regardless of the situation, growth or decline, in most cases all you can do is to look at historical trends and enrollment projections, then make your best guess regarding the upcoming year's enrollment figures. As stated earlier, the key is to take a conservative approach, which is to say you should assume revenues low and expenditures high.

Understanding your district's enrollment and the impact it will have on your budgetary decisions is vital. Seasoned superintendents realize when their districts face financial difficulties it is prudent to make changes as early possible because problems typically continue to compound. On the other side of the coin, if growth appears to be up superintendents can take comfort in knowing they are making spending decisions based upon solid data. Regardless of the situation, understanding where the ship is headed will allow you more time to think about next steps as you ponder the district's financial stability.

Annual Enrollment Projections

An annual projection focuses on the district's future enrollment estimates. These estimates allow the district's administration and school board to plan for future spending with a sense of clarity. Although the administration and board should realize they are dealing with estimates, their assumptions need to be based upon history and some prediction of future growth or decline.

In order to raise the reliability of enrollment projections, some districts choose to pay for a professionally developed demographic study; others use their own locally designed Cohort Survival Study process. Professionally developed demographic studies seem to be best because they take into account many different factors that the district is facing, or will face in the next five to ten year period. Typically you can contact either your state's school superintendents' association, or the district's architect to obtain recommendations regarding vendors for this type of study. Furthermore, if you are in a growing area, many times you can request that residential housing developers pay for a study as a way to help the district better understand its need for new schools. If you are not in a growth situation, a local service club or group of businesses may be willing to pay for the cost or other community organizations, such as the city or county government, may cooperatively fund a demographic study since these data will be of use to them as well.

Key Point #5: Consider periodically performing a professionally conducted demographic study to give you reliable and accurate data upon which to make enrollment projections.

Some districts may choose to complete their own Cohort Survival Study to track the future growth (or decline) of the district. This process is actually quite simple in that it moves each grade level up annually, estimates the size of a new kindergarten class and drops off the district's graduating seniors. Most of these studies attempt to understand what is happening as each grade level progresses through the district. As an example, does the district serve a few private schools that end at eighth grade and therefore cause each year's ninth-grade class in the high schools to grow by an additional 10 percent? It is nuances like this which districts should consider when using a Cohort Survival Study method. The Cohort Survival Study process is easy to implement and examples can be researched using most school finance texts. The challenge to a local study is that it may not take into account more complex aspects of assessing student growth. Professional demographers, when conducting a study, will take into account items such as how many home utility hook-ups were achieved in the previous year, or how many live births were observed in hospitals serving the community. Obviously, the more complex the factors considered, the more accurate the data. In some cases a more accurate assessment is needed, but in other cases, especially in stable communities, a locally designed study is just fine.

Key Point #6: If you are considering implementing a Cohort Survival Study, be sure you consult state school finance organizations or school finance texts for proper procedures and implementation strategies. These sources can help raise the reliability of your study.

The annual enrollment projection process will provide you with a picture of where the district should be headed. After a year or two you will begin to see how accurate the report is and can make modifications or adjustments as required. Regardless of whether you use it to guide the budget building process, or as a general planning tool, it can help you achieve a view of the future that would not be available otherwise.

One note of caution is that some companies will profess to be able conduct demographic studies for you, but do not employ trained demographers. They will gather various pieces of data and attempt to draw conclusions from this information, but they simply do not have the training or know-how to be effective. Superintendents should check the credentials of the firms where quotes are obtained and also speak with references, especially other school districts.

Expenditure Reports

Tracking expenditures is as important as monitoring the district's enrollment picture. To properly supervise your finance staff in this important area you should ask for a monthly expenditure report that provides data related to how the district is progressing financially.

This expenditure report should include the following four primary components:

- The current year's budget
- The current month's expenditures
- The previous year's expenditures for that month
- The amount of the budget that remains for the current budget year (both in dollars and as a percentage)

The format described above should be fairly simple for the finance office to reproduce and it ensures the ability to successfully monitor your district's expenditures. Development of the monthly expenditure report may take your finance office a bit of time to produce, but the protection it provides to you as superintendent is unmatched by other reports. Most school district finance software will produce reports that provide part of the four components, but you need to stand firm on the fact that you want this report to appear as one comprehensive document. Having all of the information described above in one report makes it much easier to read and will enhance your ability to analyze the data.

The process typically starts with you providing your finance office with an example of the components you would like in the report as outlined above. Depending upon the design of your finance system and its ease of use and capabilities, you can make a determination regarding whether the report will be developed in-house or whether a consultant is required. Regardless of the initial cost (which is always minimal) it is a report which superintendents should make nonnegotiable as it provides a simple way to monitor the district's spending.

> **Key Point #7:** Insist that your district's financial reports contain a description of the current year's budget, the current month's expenditures, the previous year's expenditures correlated to the particular month, and the percentage of the amount of the budget remaining expressed both in dollars and as a percentage.

Key Components and Their Location in the Budget Report

Here is an example of how you may choose to have your budget report organized:

Current Budget

The current year's budget is an important first component in your monthly expenditure report. It provides a benchmark regarding what the "expenditure limit" is for that particular line item. Some districts might choose to modify their report to include both the current year and the previous year's budget. This simply provides a view of how the budget has changed between the two years, which can be of use if you would like to track how the budget is changing from one year to the next.

Current Month's Expenditures

A second column in the report is the current month's expenditures. These data are obtained via the district's finance system and can be displayed in various formats, which are a function of the superintendent's choice. As an example, it might be that one superintendent wants to see the report disaggregated by program function, while another opts for individual school totals. Regardless of the format, it is important to make sure your business office can produce these data on a monthly basis.

Previous Year's Budget Data

The third column that can be represented in the report is the previous year's data for the same span of time that is covered by the current year. The goal for columns two and three is to provide a spending comparison. In most cases the report is designed to compare the two columns and then provide a percentage which points out the differences. Is the district's spending exceeding the previous year, or is it behind? Once these questions are answered you can then look for patterns and make spending decisions based upon these data.

Amount of Money Left in the Current Budget

The final column in a consolidated financial report should identify the amount of money left when comparing the budget and actual expenditures for each line item in your report. As we suggested in the information we provided earlier, it is a good idea to show this information in the form of a percentage. You can also show the remaining budget in terms of the actual dollars left in each budget category. Having both "views" enables you to quickly scan the document to determine how spending is proceeding for the current fiscal year.

In some cases, superintendents will add even more detail and design their report to identify how much of the budget was spent at that same point during the previous year. Thus, you may see that for a certain expenditure area, 65 percent of the budget is remaining, while in the previous year, 70 percent remained at that same point in time. This would obviously indicate the district, or school, is spending at an advanced rate during the current fiscal year.

Key Point #8: Be sure to include the amount of money left in the current budget on your budget reports. This figure should be expressed as a percentage but also may be expressed as a dollar amount. Some superintendents also include a comparison of the amount left in the current budget as it compares to last year's budget.

Revenue Reports

Another important part of monitoring the district's financial situation is the use of periodic revenue reports. Unlike the monthly expenditure report, revenue reports can be much harder to develop in public schools. The reason for this is that, in most cases, revenue for school districts is a function of enrollment, which is subject to some level of modification throughout the year. In some states the district's revenue picture might be set based upon enrollment figures that were generated the previous year and thus the comparison data is truly an "apples to apples" relationship. In other states these enrollment figures might not be available until late in the fiscal year or, in the most extreme cases, after the fiscal year is completed. In this situation tracking revenue might be a waste of time and thus comparing enrollment figures becomes your guide.

One concept that is consistent among most states is that districts can receive miscellaneous (locally generated) revenues, which can be tracked and truly compared on a month-to-month basis between fiscal years. Although this is typically a very small percentage of the overall budget, it can be tracked if you feel this is an item of importance.

Key Point #9: Consider tracking revenues in your budgeting process. Even though in some states revenues come at different times and on a sporadic timeline, your understanding of the exact revenues will help you in your decision making role with the board and the community.

If the decision is made to not track revenues, superintendents can take a level of comfort in following enrollment patterns as they generate the majority of the district's revenues. In other words, if enrollment exceeds the figure the district used to budget its revenues, it should exceed what was estimated in the budget, and therefore expenditure management is of greatest importance. On the other hand, if enrollment has declined as compared to the budget figure, the superintendent needs to consider how to decrease spending to make up for any potential loss.

Staffing Plans/Position Control Systems

As a fairly consistent figure, school districts across the country spend about 85 percent of their budget on salaries and benefits. Education is a labor-intensive endeavor and thus most of a school district's costs relate to its employees.

If 85 percent of the district's expenses relate to salaries and benefits, it is imperative these costs are tracked and managed effectively. To maintain a handle on these expenses, districts need to use either a staffing plan or Position Control System. It is of little consequence which process a district chooses to use and likely will be function of district size, but it is imperative that a system is in place to manage this important information. Districts need to be clear regarding how many positions are in its budget, the rate of pay for each, where these positions are coded, and finally, where these employees are physically located in the district.

It is not at all uncommon that if a district is not closely tracking their staffing situation, waste is occurring. Many times, hundreds of thousands of dollars may be spent on positions that fall through the cracks, or for salaries and benefits paid out at an inappropriate level. In fact, we believe this is the area where superintendents can obtain the greatest "bang for their buck" when putting tracking systems in place.

The staffing plan/Position Control System process should begin with an effort to obtain accurate data. Most districts maintain some sort of tracking system, even if it is an elaborate Excel spreadsheet, but the data is not always accurate. In the absence of accurate data it is very difficult to establish a baseline for the district's staffing levels. Once accuracy is achieved, the district can then design a staffing plan/Position Control System modification form. This form requires that as staffing changes are made, principals and other supervisors identify whether a new position is being formed or an existing position is being vacated. It also requires the supervisor, Human Resources (HR), and business offices be clear whether a budget adjustment will be required (the salary is increasing or decreasing as the new employee is hired).

The beauty of a staffing plan/position control system is that it ties back to the district's monthly expenditure report discussed previously. As adjustments in salaries or benefits are made, these data are then incorporated into the expenditure report so the district can be clear regarding how the budget is progressing throughout the school year.

Consider the following tips as you help the district "stay afloat" financially:

- Stand firm with your departments regarding development of the four identified reports. The district may have other reports it has used in the past and you will need to analyze each to determine whether they provide the data described in this section.
- Be sure to specify how often you expect to receive each report.

- Establish benchmarks with your departments regarding when the district should become concerned with the data. As an example, once expenditures reach the 92 percent level for the district, you will meet with the finance staff to discuss potential safeguards.

LONG-RANGE FINANCIAL PROJECTION: YOUR OWN CRYSTAL BALL

One of the most important tools that superintendents can implement in their districts is the use of a long-range financial planning process. As the heading states, this process allows you the ability to see into the future with a "crystal ball." In essence, a long-range financial projection employs a complex mix of assumptions in designing a predictive model related to the district's finances over a period of time (typically three to five years). This predictive model considers the district's enrollment trends and makes assumptions regarding revenue, expenditures, and staffing levels. These assumptions are placed into an intricate spreadsheet and the result is a set of predictions related to the district's fund balance over the next three to five year period.

The Importance of Long-Range Projection

One reason this is such an important tool is that it enables districts to make better financial decisions. If enrollment is decreasing and cuts are required, the district can run scenarios and design solutions using the long-range financial projection system. Conversely, if the district is growing, it can add new schools to its financial projection, which provides a clearer picture related to future operational costs.

Obviously long-range financial projection systems are only as good as the assumptions upon which they are built. It is important for districts to maintain accurate data in the areas that most substantially impact the financial projection system. It is not uncommon for districts to use their long-range financial projection system to plan their budget for the coming year, or determine the need for an operating levy. Additionally, as the district engages in the strategic planning process, it can use its long-range financial planning tool to understand the impact of the plan. Use of a long-range financial planning system to provide clarity in the strategic planning process is a step that districts rarely consider but, when implemented, can pay huge dividends. Adding this step shows the board, administration, staff, and community that you are a superintendent who is a prudent decision maker and that you are focused on proper due diligence.

Key Point #10: Use long-range planning to provide clarity and predictability in the budgeting process.

Districts have a couple of options when it comes to using long-range financial projection systems. The district may choose to work with a vendor in its state that has designed a system for school use, or it may design its own system. Regardless of which direction the district decides to proceed, the primary concern is that a system is chosen which offers data upon which long-range financial decisions can be made and scenarios run.

The introduction of a long-range financial planning system to your district is not only a wise move, but one that shows your prowess regarding financial management. Although you were most likely hired as the superintendent based upon your ability to convince the board of your potential to improve student achievement, if you don't quickly get a handle on the district's financial picture you could end up experiencing a great deal of difficulty.

Consider the following regarding long-range financial projection:

- Ask your board to assist district staff in selecting which assumptions to use in the long-range financial projection system. This ensures everyone is on the same page, thus blame cannot be inappropriately placed on any one individual at a later point in time.
- Use your long-range financial projection to inform the budget development process.
- Promote use of the long-range financial projection system as a guide in the strategic planning process.

UNDERSTANDING THE SCHOOL DISTRICT'S FINANCIAL AUDIT

Every school district goes through an annual financial audit but in most cases the information gathered and presented by the auditing firm is not clearly understood. Many superintendents and school boards politely listen to the audit presentation, accept the report, and quickly move on to the next agenda topic. Unless the auditor or the district's business official raises a concern, few comments are made regarding this very important report. Unfortunately, as stated earlier, most superintendents and school boards lack an understanding of what the audit report is truly indicating.

Unless someone has a finance background, or has been "trained" regarding what to look for in the audit report, they are at a loss when trying to decipher its complexity. In other cases you might have a school board member with a finance background, but no training regarding "governmental accounting" (fund accounting) practices. Most individuals who have received finance training are taught to understand profit and loss accounting, which is different from governmental accounting.

> **Key Point #11:** Spend some time with officials from the firm conducting your audit (the audit manager or partner is best) to ask the question: "What should I understand about this year's audit?"

It is important for superintendents to have a basic understanding of the audit process. In concept, an audit consists of the district preparing its financial statements for review by the district's auditor. The auditor provides an "opinion" regarding the accuracy of the district's financial statements and then prepares a report for the board. Auditors are assumed to be "independent" of the district and therefore the board trusts their report as an objective measure of the district's financial condition. The audit process also enables the board to, at least in part, fulfill its fiduciary responsibility to the district's taxpayers.

What should superintendents look for when reviewing the district's audit? In a report titled *Fiscal Fitness: A Guide to Your School District's Budget* (found at http://www.emsc.nysed.gov/mgtserv/FiscalFitnessGuide.htm), the New York State Department of Education poses five key questions which provide a framework for understanding the audit. We have adapted these questions, narrowing them to four (shown below) which enable the superintendent to conduct a management level review of their district's financial health. Most school districts hire a business official to oversee the intricacies of the district's finances, but superintendents must understand and be able to explain the big picture.

Four key questions for superintendents to ask related to the auditing process are the following:

- Did the district end the year with a surplus or deficit with its revenues and expenditures?
- What trends are observable when comparing revenues and expenditures over time?
- What are the reasons for significant variances that occurred between the district's budget as amended, if applicable, and actual revenues and expenditures?

- How much is in the district's General Fund fund balance (savings) account? Has the district been adding to or depleting this account in the past three to five years?

Let's look at each of the major questions in more detail.

- Did the district end the year with a surplus or deficit with its revenues and expenditures?

    In most cases this information will be found in the management report of the audit, but further details are available in the audit report itself. Reviewing this information allows superintendents to observe the effectiveness of the district's fiscal controls. If revenues were understated in the budget one should ask what caused this situation. Did the district end up with increased enrollment? Was specific revenue not accounted for in the budget? The same types of questions must be posed regarding the district's expenditures. If the district overspent its expenditure budget superintendents should ask how this was allowed to happen. Were proper controls not in place? Was there some sort of unexpected event? The same line of questioning should be considered if the district underestimated its revenues or expenditures. Is the business office budgeting too conservatively? Did a large expenditure not come to pass?

    The key in this area is to not only understand whether the district under- or overestimated its revenues and expenditures, but to ask intuitive questions regarding what transpired. In most cases logical explanations exist for why a certain outcome was experienced. Superintendents who ask questions increase accountability, which enhances the district's financial stability.

- What trends are observable when comparing revenues and expenditures over time?

    Trend data is important to review as it can highlight patterns that would not be otherwise identified. It is always good to look at the previous year's data, but reviewing up to five years of information is preferable. This review allows you to begin asking critical questions: Are the district's expenditures outpacing its revenues? Why are revenues decreasing? What is causing expenditures to expand at such an explosive rate?

    This type of questioning allows superintendents and business officials alike to understand what types of adjustments might be required. It also encourages the district to analyze whether previous audit information has had an impact on the fiscal operation. As initial questions are answered they typically identify additional concerns that should be addressed. A thorough review of trends on an annual basis enables superintendents to understand where the district is headed.

- What are the reasons for significant variances that occurred between the district's budget as amended, if applicable, and actual revenues and expenditures?

    Districts typically amend their budgets multiple times during the fiscal year. One of these amendments may come late in the school year in an effort to "match" the budget with actual revenue and expenditure data.

    If, when reviewing the audit, you observe a wide variance between the budget and actual expenditures, further investigation is required. Did the district not make a spring amendment to its budget? Did it make an amendment, but unforeseen circumstances arose? Regardless, this is an issue that should be reviewed by superintendents, and if wide variation is apparent, questions must be asked. We believe acceptable variation would fall between 1 and 2 percent (1 percent or less is optimum) when comparing the budget to actual expenditures. If the district's audit reflects a variance outside this range, superintendents should discuss potential reasons with their business office staff.

- How much is in the district's General Fund fund balance (savings) account? Has the district been adding to or depleting this account in the past three to five years?

    This is likely the most significant measure of your school district's financial health. The General Fund is where most school district salaries and benefits are budgeted, and accounts for between 80 and 90 percent of the district's total expenses. As stated above it is important to analyze whether the fund balance has been growing or decreasing. Regardless, can you answer why? What actions must be considered based upon these data? It is important to realize that although a decrease in fund balance is normally a negative situation (unless it is a planned spend down of funds), an increase can also point to a problem. If your budget predicted a certain fund balance and the district exceeds that figure, you might be open to public and employee scrutiny.

    It is also important to keep an eye on other fund balance accounts. In most states school districts have some flexibility regarding how certain fund balances are used and thus, in combination these accounts, can have a positive impact on the General Fund. Developing a plan for the level of fund balance that the school district will maintain is an important decision. Conventional wisdom is that districts should keep at least a 5 percent fund balance in their General Fund, although this may be impacted by state regulation or size of the district.

Consider the following tips regarding analyzing your district's financial audit:

- Remember to read the management report component of your district's audit on an annual basis.
- Plan to meet with the audit firms manager or partner for your audit to ask: What should I understand about this year's audit?
- Be aware of the fact that although some board members understand finance, they likely have little knowledge of governmental accounting practices.
- Be sure to review the management and audit report at the conclusion of the district's annual audit and apply the four questions provided above. Use your analysis to ask the district's finance staff intuitive questions about the state of district's financial health.

SUMMARY

Understanding and being able to monitor the budget of a school district is a complex, yet essential skill for a new superintendent. Even though each state's process is slightly different there are some core reports that can help you stay in the know. As you think about the content you've learned in this chapter, reflect on the following questions:

- What are the four key reports you need to have your finance department develop to keep you informed about the school district's financial status?
- Why is keeping a close eye on enrollment essential for you as the superintendent?
- What questions should you ask the firm auditing your school district?
- What is the role of long-range planning in the school district financial management process?

Even though effective budget management is one key to your success, how you move new ideas and initiatives forward initially is crucial. In the next chapter, How to Implement New Ideas in Your Initial Years as Superintendent, we will give you ideas and strategies to help you successfully realize the kinds of changes you were hired by your board to implement.

5

How to Implement New Ideas in Your Initial Years as Superintendent

> *For every failure, there's an alternative course of action. You just have to find it. When you come to a roadblock, take a detour.*
>
> —Mary Kay Ash

One area of concern for new superintendents over the years has been the perception by employees and parents that he or she is moving forward with his or her own agenda without taking into consideration the district's strengths, needs, or past successes. In the book *Becoming a Superintendent: Challenges of School District Leadership,* author Carolyn Chapman (1997) highlights some of the major reasons new superintendents ran into trouble or lost their jobs in a study called the Beginning Superintendent Study (BSS). One of the major causes is pointed out in the following:

A new superintendent, who was terminated at the end of his first year, was bold enough to reflect on some of his misadventures. He pointed out that his primary mistake was "overplanning and trying to accomplish [his] plans in too short a time period." When he took over the district he perceived a district in deep trouble, and he saw his role as getting it out of trouble as quickly as possible. Thus he became Harold Hill, the legendary bandleader in *The Music Man,* high stepping down Main Street in River City, Iowa. The problem was that none of the 76 trombones were behind him, so he waved his baton and stepped smartly out front, becoming a one-man parade as everyone else sat on the curb watching. (Chapman, 1997)

The experience of this superintendent matches the experiences of several of the colleagues we have worked with over the years. Many superintendents get themselves in trouble by moving forward on initiatives before the rest of the school district is ready.

ABOUT THIS CHAPTER

Successfully moving forward on changes and new initiatives requires that you take the time to build a base of understanding and commitment in relation to the change or implementation. In this chapter, you will learn the following about the change process and how to use this knowledge to bring forth new ideas while honoring past accomplishments and people's feelings:

- Change process basics
- Taking advantage of your honeymoon period
- Transitions and the change process
- Gardner's Levers of Change
- Guskey's Teacher Change Process
- How to facilitate groups through change
- Dealing with Implementation Blockers

Handling the transition to a new leader can be very difficult for a school district and its stakeholders. See how Lois, a new superintendent, worked with this situation in one district:

After Lois accepted the job as superintendent of Promising School District, she decided to spend time getting to know the community and its needs. She instituted a variety of public information gathering sessions to learn more about the district. These were events that were purposely scheduled to help her meet and listen to small groups of people in settings that were comfortable for them. She went to workplaces, service clubs, neighborhood gatherings, community picnics, and other events and asked people to respond to a questionnaire she had designed. The questionnaire asked people two simple questions: What do you like about the district and what do you think needs to be changed? She constantly asked the people that she met these questions and wrote down their responses.

After three to four months of gathering data, Lois shared the information she had gathered with the public through a board presentation, in a newspaper article she wrote for the local paper, in the school district newsletter, and during service club presentations. She formed a small task force to look into the ideas that she had gathered and developed a plan about what to do as a result of all of these data. The task force came up with several strategies to help the district move forward.

In looking at what Lois did in this situation, she was able to come into the district, gather data, and listen to others before presenting a plan of her own. Lois had some ideas of how she wanted to move forward with the district, but temporarily suspended her opinions in order to truly listen to what others had to say. She did what Peter Senge refers to as "building meaning into the vision" (Senge, 1989).

In many instances, new superintendents fail to build the kind of support and involvement that Lois did in her position. Look at the situation that Ken, another new superintendent, caused by moving forward too fast and having limited support for the new ideas he was trying to institute:

Ken wanted to implement a new accountability process in the district where he had just started to work. He had several communications with board members and his board chair, who were pushing the new accountability process. The board had felt that the teachers and administrators were not being held accountable for student achievement issues in the district. Ken worked on a plan and unveiled it to the board during a special meeting they held in early October. His administrative staff and the teachers in the district were unaware of the plan until they saw it in the board meeting agenda that was posted before the meeting. Several representatives of the teachers' association were in the audience and voiced concerns with the plan and the board allowed them to speak on the issue. The board directed Ken to get feedback about the plan from teachers and administrators in the district and then report back to the board at its meeting in November. As Ken traveled around to various buildings to talk about the potential plan, his ideas were met with resistance. Teachers even engaged in a phone calling campaign to inundate board members with complaints. At the November board meeting, the teachers' association voiced additional concerns about the plan. The board chair moved and the rest of the board voted to table the plan, and told the superintendent that he should have put together a more "thoughtful" process.

In this example, Ken fell into a common trap that plagues new superintendents in regard to bringing forth ideas and possible changes to a school district. He failed to get staff involvement and engagement in developing his new plan. Once it had been introduced, he had to fight an uphill battle to try and convince people to "buy into" it. He mistakenly put his stock in thinking the board would back him even though the staff was not in favor of the plan. When the staff began to resist the new plan and put pressure on the board, the members folded and left Ken "holding the bag" and taking the blame for the failure. In some cases, superintendents can survive a minor incident such as this and become successful. In other cases, however, these types of incidents set a tone that can lead to his or her downfall.

> **Key Point #1:** Take time to understand the change process and the idea of building meaning for the vision before moving into a major change as the superintendent.

THE CHANGE PROCESS

Much has been written about the change process over the years so we won't go into great detail on it in this section. During our preparation as administrators we were introduced to two general ideas regarding change in organizations. They were:

1. As a new leader, come in and make as many changes as possible and get them over with during your first year. Once you have accomplished this, you will have all of the changes behind you and then you can do other things.
2. During your first year as leader, work to get to know the strengths and limitations of the organization before making changes.

From our experiences in schools and districts and in the superintendency, we recommend that as the new superintendent you focus on the second general change theory where you take time, get to know the organization, its people, and its strengths and weaknesses before moving forward on a major change project.

> **Key Point #2:** Take time to build relationships and an understanding of the school district's needs and assets before launching a major initiative by yourself. Make sure you have engaged the support of key groups and individuals before moving forward.

The Honeymoon Period

The period between when you start a job and when people expect you to begin implementation of your agenda is called the honeymoon period of your leadership. We didn't provide a timeline for the honeymoon period because it can vary depending on how quickly you need to move forward. Normally, during the honeymoon period you can get away with some mistakes because people think you are just learning about the district. Once your honeymoon period is over, people start to judge you based on their expectations for performance. Many superintendents use this honeymoon period to learn about the school district and the needs that it has, while others just move forward with implementing the kinds of changes they feel the district needs in order to be effective. A common criticism that is thrust upon leaders is that they made a change without really getting to know the people and the needs of the school district. Great superintendents know how to use the honeymoon period to maximize their information gathering and planning for implementation of change in the district. These kinds of superintendents actually plan their honeymoon period using strategies similar to those contained in the following honeymoon planning guide.

Use the guide in Figure 5.1 to help you maximize your learning during the honeymoon period. Periodically review it for changes and adjustments.

Figure 5.1 Honeymoon Planning Guide

As you enter this new position, rate your impressions of the operating condition of the following district departments:

School board/community relations
☐ Operating effectively   ☐ Needs minor refinements   ☐ Needs major attention

Custodial/maintenance program
☐ Operating effectively   ☐ Needs minor refinements   ☐ Needs major attention

Instructional/assessment program
☐ Operating effectively   ☐ Needs minor refinements   ☐ Needs major attention

Food service program
☐ Operating effectively   ☐ Needs minor refinements   ☐ Needs major attention

Transportation program
☐ Operating effectively   ☐ Needs minor refinements   ☐ Needs major attention

HR department
☐ Operating effectively   ☐ Needs minor refinements   ☐ Needs major attention

Employee contracts
☐ Operating effectively   ☐ Needs minor refinements   ☐ Needs major attention

---

(Continued)

Figure 5.1 (Continued)

Of the items above that you rated as "needs major attention," how urgent are the needs and how soon do you need to address them?

(Item 1) _____

❏ Not urgent

❏ Very Urgent—Needs to be addressed by _____

(Item 2) _____

❏ Not urgent

❏ Very Urgent—Needs to be addressed by _____

(Item 3) _____

❏ Not urgent

❏ Very Urgent—Needs to be addressed by _____

(Item 4) _____

❏ Not urgent

❏ Very Urgent—Needs to be addressed by _____

Of the items that you rated as "operating effectively" and "needs minor refinements," what data do you need to learn more about these programs? How do you plan to gather this information? List a timeline for gathering this information.

Items	Additional Data Needed	Plan to Gather Data	Timeline

Detail how you will use your honeymoon period to help you gather the information you need in order to learn as much as possible about the district, its people, and its future needs.

Key Point #3: Develop a plan to utilize your "honeymoon" period to gain a better understanding of your district and maximize your change agenda.

TRANSITIONS AND THE CHANGE PROCESS

Author William Bridges (1991) in his book *Managing Transitions: Making The Most of Change.* focuses on how we manage the transitions that occur when moving from present conditions to the new change. Transitions can be difficult for people involved in change efforts simply because of the nature of transitions. In a transition, people are between their old way of thinking and the new behavior. Bridges contends that during the transition people become uncomfortable because of the loss of control they have during this period. The diagram in Figure 5.2 sums up the transition phase.

As superintendents we need to help people work through this transition stage in order to assist them as they move through the change process.

LEVERS OF CHANGE

Howard Gardner offers another perspective on change. In his book *Changing Minds* (2004), he talks about some of the attributes that need to be in place to help others (and ourselves) to change our minds, a necessary step in working through change. Gardner identifies what he calls "levers" to help cause mind changes to occur. These levers are the following:

- Reason
- Research

Figure 5.2 The Gap or Transition in the Change Process

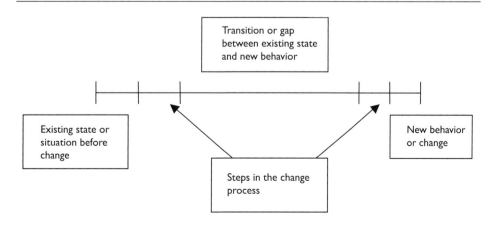

- Resonance
- Representational redescriptions
- Resources and rewards
- Real world events
- Resistances

Let's take a closer look at these levers and their meaning in the change process.

Reason: Gardner contends that we use reason in making the decision to change our minds and ultimately move through the change process. As we are exposed to a new idea, we evaluate the idea on its merit and whether or not it makes good sense to us.

Strategies to help you implement the lever of reason: As we propose changes we must let people know the logic behind the change. We must also give them a chance to begin to see the change and apply their own logic to it.

Research: With the lever of reason, people going through a change will attempt to gather data about the change. They want to see research and testimonials touting the new idea or practice.

Strategies to help you implement the lever of research: As a new superintendent you should provide a good rationale for a proposed change to the staff members in your district. You can also provide articles and other research that show how the new idea of behavior will positively impact their professional practice. Having people visit other districts (possibly including one where you worked in the past) to actually see the new idea or practice in place and gather testimonials of how it's worked will help your group see the new idea is related to research.

Resonance: The principle of resonance relates to the people engaged in the change effort having a "feeling" or intuition that the new idea or behavior makes sense.

Strategies to help you implement the lever of resonance: Help people get a "feel" for the change. As you meet with small groups to talk about the change or the need for the use of new ideas, have them do a "gut check" related to the implementation. Ask your staff to meet in pairs and talk about their emotional reactions to the change. Have them share ideas and strategies. Let them experience emotional situations related to the change, such as student and teacher testimonials, to help them feel the change.

Representational redescriptions: Even though this term sounds complex, its meaning is fairly simple and straight-forward; it simply means that the new idea or concept needs to be seen by people in a variety of learning modalities.

Strategies to help you implement the lever of representation redescriptions: In addition to hearing about the change, it is also necessary for people to see the change presented in a visual mode. You might consider having people make a collage or sculpture representing the new idea or behavior. The visual representation strategy shared below would be a good activity to use in helping people examine the change or new idea from a variety of perspectives.

Application Activity: Visual Representation

This activity relates to Gardner's lever, representational redescriptions. One way for a group to truly "see" the change and develop emotional understandings is to have them construct visual representations or sculptures depicting the new idea or change. Here is how it can work in a group:

- Divide the larger group into smaller teams of three to six members.

- Provide chart paper, markers, pipe cleaners, ribbon, cardboard tubes, and other "craft" material to each small team.

- Assign the teams to construct a visual representation, sculpture, or other object that captures the essence of the change or new idea. Give the groups five to ten minutes to complete their constructions.

- At the end of the construction phase ask each team to share their product with the larger group. Make sure the teams explain their representation and provide clarification for the larger group.

- Ask team members to talk about what they learned as a result of the activity.

(Adapted from Eller & Eller, 2006)

Authors' Note: John recently used this activity with a group that was going to change the focus of their site-based decision making program. The school district was hosting an open meeting with members of the community and employees in the district. The larger group was divided into several small groups. Each small group was given a box of random materials (sequins, feathers, markers, cardboard tubes, buttons, pipe cleaners, etc.). The small groups actually built sculptures that represented the change in their program. Each group presented its sculpture and explained how it illustrated the new change. All the groups were permitted to walk around and look at the other sculptures in detail. Most of the participants at the session rated this activity as a helpful way for them to work through the change.

Resources and rewards: In many instances change can be facilitated by the rewards people get from it or the resources in place to help them implement the change. Resources and rewards can be a powerful lever to facilitate change.

Strategies to help you implement the lever of resources and rewards: When thinking about implementing a change, it is a good idea to do a cost-benefit analysis of the change. This helps you and your staff to actually see what will be involved with the change. When you start to plan a change project, the Cost-Benefit Planning Template in Figure 5.3 will help you.

Figure 5.3 Cost-Benefit Planning Template

Describe in detail the change you are planning to implement:

_____

_____

_____

_____

List the subcomponents and objectives needed to implement this change:

_____

_____

_____

_____

Subcomponents	Cost of Implementing (all costs including human resources and time)	Benefits of Implementing
1.		
2.		
3.		
4.		
5.		
6.		
Totals		

Examine both the cost and benefit columns. If the benefits outweigh the costs, you will probably be successful in helping others see the importance of implementing the change. If the costs outweigh the benefits, you may have trouble selling the idea or you may need to remove other initiatives or add incentives to help people consider making the change.

Be sure to identify any rewards or resources you could implement to assist people in making the change. In putting together a successful change process, a colleague of ours instituted several major incentives to successfully change the teaching behaviors in his school district.

Julio, the superintendent of a metropolitan school district, wanted the teachers to meet the needs of their English Language Learners (ELL) more successfully. He put monetary resources into curriculum reforms and high-quality training programs to help his teachers clearly understand skills they would need to implement in their classrooms to ensure the ELL students could improve their achievement. He also allocated money to hire language and math coaches in each building to help the teachers receive instruction and support to learn and implement the new teaching strategies. Finally, he designated a late start to the school day every Wednesday to provide teachers with collaboration and planning time to work together to design quality instruction to help the students be successful. The school district had to move money from other programs to make all of this work, but in the end the teachers had most of the resources they needed in order to move successfully through the change. He had to take some public pressure at the start of this program, but as student achievement improved he received more and more public support for the way he focused resources on the most immediate problem faced in the district and the changes he implemented that enabled the teachers to be successful with their students.

Sample Incentives to Help Teachers Implement Changes

Here are a few of the many incentives you can use as a superintendent to help teachers be successful in implementing new ideas:

- Public recognition
- Release time
- Reducing another task in order to allow them to focus on the new change
- Support staff at the building level to assist them with learning new behaviors
- Monetary rewards (staff bonuses, merit pay, etc.)
- Extra professional travel
- Reduced duties

(Continued)

Sample Incentives to Help Teachers Implement Changes (Continued)

- Coupons and reductions for purchases, dining, etc., in the local area
- Leadership positions within the school district
- Occasional class coverage
- Materials and supplies
- Opportunities to present at conferences
- Reduced teaching load

Real world events: In many change efforts, some large-scale event has been the spark behind the change. These events can be localized or national in scope.

> In one school district a colleague of ours, Ann, experienced an influx of new families in her district because several new high-tech companies moved into the area. The parents that worked at these companies had high expectations and were very involved with their children's education. The school district had to increase the number of advanced placement offerings, which required teachers to learn new strategies and ideas. Ann gathered information about the expectations of these parents and their companies, and communicated these to the teachers as she prepared to implement the changes needed to help these students be successful. She was able to use the lever of real world events to help the teachers move forward on the change.

Strategies to help you implement the lever of real world events: In this area, you have to be careful when communicating the change from the outside world to the teachers. If you are not careful, you can sound like "Chicken Little" proclaiming that the sky is falling. Experienced teachers probably have heard the "gloom and doom" speech several times over their careers. We have been successful in bringing along a smaller group of informal leaders and helping them to understand the change in the outside world first, then bringing the rest of the staff along a little later. In the example above about Ann's change effort, she took some of her informal teacher leaders with her to the initial meetings she had with the new companies. These teachers saw firsthand what was coming and helped her sell the idea to the other teachers. These informal leaders were talking about the needed changes and Ann followed up their message with strategies and support.

The change still took considerable effort but Ann noticed fewer problems than she had experienced in other change efforts in the past because she was able to help her teachers understand the need for the change.

Resistances: According to Gardner, the levers listed above all work to help reduce people's resistance to change. The time when people have the least resistance to change is early in their lives. As they get older, they become more resistant to change. This concept is related to some of the work we have done regarding "frames of reference." The concept is based on the work of Thomas Kuhn (who originally looked at how scientific concepts were "discovered" in his landmark book, *The Structure of Scientific Revolutions*, 1962). Basically his work outlined how people came to a certain way of thinking about a topic or idea. In the groups we have been helping through the change process over the years, we have developed an adaptation of the process of working through resistance based on Kuhn's general principles. The following model has been helpful in our understanding of how people develop resistance to new ideas and changes. As you review the following stages, think about how they apply to people you have seen who exhibit resistance to change.

Frames of Reference Related to the Change Process

People normally experience the following stages as they come to understand the world around them.

- A person experiences a way of doing their job or a set of tasks.
- After a time, their mind begins to draw cause-effect conclusions related to the way they perform the task or tasks.
- As they continue to do the tasks, their mind begins to form a frame of reference around the task; they notice a positive effect as a result of the way they do a task.
- Since they see positive results related to how they perform the tasks, they begin to feel comfortable with their competence with their strategies for task completion. At this point, they are almost on automatic pilot when doing the tasks.
- A change is introduced to their environment that may require them to change how they perform the tasks (some of these changes fit into Gardner's levers).
- Since the change requires new skills that may not fit into their frame of reference for how they have implemented the tasks in the past, their mind goes into denial; they begin to deny that a change is needed on their part and instead may insist that the problem lies outside of them. They will take incoming information related to the change and "bend" this information to reinforce their previous way of performing the tasks. This is the place where leaders typically "push" or try to force compliance with the

change. This behavior only makes the resistance stronger. Until the frame of reference has a chance to be weakened and changed, these people will not move forward on the new change.

- Finally, after some time has passed, people have had a chance to see the new idea in operation, looked at examples where the ideas worked well, and come to make the change or strategies more personal to them; their frame of reference begins to shift toward the new change. At this point, they are able to begin embracing the new idea and learning new strategies. They start to form a new frame of reference around the new idea and the process begins again. (Information adapted from *The Structure of Scientific Revolutions* by Thomas Kuhn, 1962)

The crucial time around this resistance is during the time when people are moving from comfort with the old idea to accepting the new idea or change. We have to support them during this time and provide multiple ways for them to interact with the new behaviors/ideas in a non-threatening manner. John had a recent experience that illustrates this idea:

In one school district, John worked with a high school staff to implement a set of student learning standards. In his initial interactions with the staff he encountered lots of open resistance to the new standards. Instead of digging in on the program, he listened to the concerns, validated those that made sense, and provided lots of opportunities over the next year for teachers to see and interact with the components of the standards program in a variety of different forms. In each of the sessions offered there were people present who were openly resistant to the program, but John noticed over time there was less and less open resistance. Either the really vocal people stopped coming or some of them began to accept the new ideas. John was very careful not to attack dissenters in his interactions with the faculty. Over the year, more and more of the teachers began to try new ideas in their classrooms. After a time, some of these teachers began to get more vocal in meetings, expressing that the new ideas were not hard to integrate into their existing units and topics. The staff began to accept the new ideas and utilize them in their classrooms.

Obviously much more care and work went into this change effort than can be summed up in a short paragraph. The main point of the example was to show that if people are supported and helped to move along, they would begin to accept new ideas and change their frames of reference. In the example you noticed the teachers began to implement and try out ideas in their classrooms before talking about their positive feelings in the group sessions. This mirrors research by Thomas Guskey (2000) that shows

Figure 5.4 Guskey's Teacher Change Process

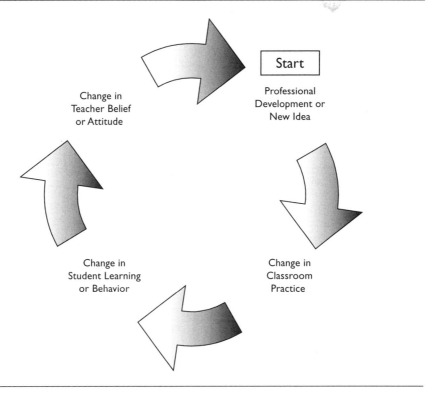

SOURCE: Based on the work of Guskey, 2000, p. 139.

teachers change their practices first, and then begin to change their attitudes about new instructional practices. Figure 5.4 illustrates this process.

The figure shows the following steps:

- A new idea or concept is introduced to a teacher or group or teachers.
- The teacher or group of teachers tries out the idea in their classroom(s).
- If they find the idea works, they will want to learn more information about the foundations behind the idea.
- A change in attitude will occur related to the new idea or concept.

Guskey's change cycle reinforces the importance of providing clear, strategy-based staff development and implementation assistance in the early phases of change. As the superintendent, you may not hear glowing remarks about the new idea or concept until people have had a chance to try it out and evaluate it in their classrooms. This is another reason to make sure you move forward on a change effort with others.

Strategies to Consider When Dealing With Resistance

- Present the components of the new idea or change in small groups; encourage people to come up with a list of concerns related to the new idea, work off this list, and try to address concerns as you move forward
- Use a group of informal leaders to help you make the new ideas understandable and real; have this group do some of the communicating with the entire faculty
- Keep in mind the principle of buy in; overcoming resistance involves working through concerns and getting buy in
- Present the stages of change from Figure 5.3 or the model from Figure 5.4 to the group; by sharing the stages typically experienced by others, you help them see they are like others who have worked through major changes. When groups feel "normal" their level of concerns goes down and they are more able to concentrate on managing their emotions during the change

FACILITATING/GUIDING GROUPS THROUGH CHANGE

We have found the use of facilitation activities has helped groups successfully work through the stages of the change process. Below are a few ideas we have found helpful with employee groups.

Putting It Behind Us

In *Energizing Staff Meetings* (Eller & Eller, 2006), many ideas are presented that help groups work through the change process. Putting It Behind Us has been used successfully to help people let go of old behaviors and ideas and begin to move forward. Here is a brief explanation of the activity from the book:

Because teachers can be especially fond of holding on to old instructional practices or materials after a new curriculum is adopted, this strategy can help them to emotionally detach from their old practices. Ceremonies and processes help people move beyond their existing comfort zone to new ways of doing business. Here are the steps to make this strategy work:

1. Talk with the staff about the importance of moving beyond the old practice and the need to look at new ideas.
2. Let the group know you think it is important for them to have a chance to emotionally process the change in practices from the old to the new.

3. On a piece of chart paper, write down the existing or old practice. Divide the paper into two columns; designate one column for the positives of the old practice, the other for the negatives of the old practice.

4. Have the entire group engage in brainstorming ideas for both columns. You can have people meet in small groups first or open up the floor to ideas from the group.

5. After all of the brainstormed ideas have been written on the chart, ask the larger group to divide itself into small teams of three or four people to talk about the process and the ideas generated during the exercise.

6. On chart paper, list the new innovation or practice to be implemented; list the same two columns that were listed on the first chart; positive attributes of the new practice and negative attributes of the new practice.

7. Ask the group to brainstorm ideas to fill the chart.

8. Have the groups compare the two charts; look for similarities and differences.

9. Physically place the old chart in the back of the room and the new chart in the front. Ask the group to brainstorm ideas that deal with the negatives identified on the new chart. Ask the group to talk about what was learned in the process. (From Eller & Eller, 2006, p. 133)

Another idea we have used successfully is based on the activity the "Learning Walk."

Learning Walk

Recently many authors have commented about the relationship between learning and movement. This strategy allows you to capitalize on movement and helps people think about and understand the new idea or change. Follow these steps:

- Have the group members stand up.
- Direct them to find a partner with whom they can go on a learning walk with during the next two or three minutes.
- As they walk, ask the pairs to talk about the significant aspects they understand in relation to the change process. Have them talk about how the new idea or innovation might be implemented and what barriers to success they see possibly getting in the way.
- When the group comes back together, let each pair share the major points of their small-group discussions. After all of the small groups have had a chance to present their findings, hold a

conversation with the entire group about what trends or similar ideas they noticed that were common to the entire large group.

Talking and movement assists people to verbalize their concerns about a change and work through some of the issues associated with the change. This strategy may not solve all your problems, but it does help people vent then calm down and truly begin to understand the specific issues related to the new idea or change.

IMPLEMENTATION BLOCKING

In any change effort there are people in your district that are very resistant because they are in some way benefiting from the present way business is being conducted. When they see a change on the horizon, they see that their advantage or benefit from the status quo is going to evaporate. At times these people are very vocal about their opposition to the change; at other times, they are subtler. A subtle way some of these resistant people try to make you abandon your change ideas is to use a technique we have come to call Implementation Blocking.

The concept of implementation blocking is an effort of a person or group of people to undermine your confidence in moving forward on a change effort through comments meant to make you think there is widespread and powerful opposition to the change or that there is a major lack of logic involved in the change effort. Their objective is to get you to doubt your plan or reason for the change and make a decision to abandon your effort.

Here are some of the examples we have seen recently used by Implementation Blockers:

- "Many of the parents that have talked to me have concerns about this idea."
- "Several board members have expressed their doubts about this project."
- "Many staff members have told me in confidence that they are opposed to this idea."
- "Surely a person of your skill and experience has some doubts about the structure of this program."
- "As you logically have thought through this plan, you must have identified the potential problems of this idea since you have so much experience as a school leader."

To deal effectively with Implementation Blockers you need to identify that the process is occurring and stop your brain from beginning to play the "self doubt" tape that is almost automatically turned on in our heads. Keep these points in mind as you experience Implementation Blockers:

- Listen to the message being presented by the suspected Implementation Blocker, ask clarification questions, and seek to understand the nature and origin of the concern.
- Listen for the core of the concern and rephrase it back to the sender to check on its accuracy.
- Listen for specific language; be careful when you hear vague or general statements; ask questions that require the Implementation Blocker to be specific about the alleged concerns and their sources.
- Think through the conversation; avoid feeling bad while seeking to understand the power and size of the dissenting group.
- Do a reality check with trusted colleagues and staff members; listen carefully and try to learn about things that may need to be changed or adjusted with the implementation.

SUMMARY

In this chapter we have discussed some of the elements relating to change and the strategies and ideas you can implement as a new superintendent to help you as you work with people on the change process. As you reflect back on the major points presented, think about how you would answer the following questions:

- What is meant by the term honeymoon; how can you maximize your success utilizing this concept?
- How do the levers of change identified by Gardner impact or influence change processes proposed by superintendents?
- How do Implementation Blockers work to slow down the pace of change? What are some effective ways to deal with these types of people?
- What is a relationship between frames of reference and people's ability to make changes?

Change can be difficult for all parties involved. As a new superintendent you are experiencing massive changes in how you operate as a leader. One of the ways your success is measured is by how skillfully you help people work through and implement new ideas and changes. Keep the elements presented in this chapter in mind as you tackle this difficult and challenging role.

In the next chapter, Supervising Principals and Directors: Strategies for Success, you will learn ideas to help you as you work with your directors and principals to provide them with support and guidance. Use the activities and strategies you learn as you work with these important people.

6

Supervising Principals and Directors

Strategies for Success

The first responsibility of a leader is to define reality. The last is to say thank you. In between, the leader is a servant.
—Max De Pree

As a new superintendent you will be responsible for the supervision and evaluation of subordinates. Some of these subordinates include principals, directors, assistant superintendents, division managers, and others in charge of certain parts of school district operations. Many new superintendents find this to be a hard assignment since they normally have not had extensive experiences in the areas where they are charged with the task of supervision.

ABOUT THIS CHAPTER

Since many superintendents come to the job having been building principals, most have had a chance to supervise others. A key difference in the supervision duties of a superintendent is that the scope of job responsibilities is much wider. The people who do the various jobs in a school district have diverse ways of thinking and processing, plus they do a variety of very different jobs. Many superintendents need some assistance or guidance in learning how to supervise these diverse employees during the initial stages of their superintendency.

In this chapter you will learn strategies and ideas for effective supervision of subordinates, including the following:

- Supervision of key administrative staff to include those at the executive level and principals
- Strategies for supervising directors and department/divisional leaders
- Performance reviews for department heads, assistant superintendents, and directors
- How to set goals with administrative staff

SUPERVISION OF EXECUTIVE-LEVEL ADMINISTRATORS AND PRINCIPALS

As a new superintendent, even though you work directly with the board and get much of your power from that relationship, you need to implement supervision strategies that will assist you in building professional relationships with your principals, directors, and other supervisory staff. Many times these people have been in the school district much longer than you or previous superintendents, carry considerable clout with the community, and talk to many people about your leadership. From our experiences over the years, we have found that most people working at the supervisory level in a school district are looking for the following from their superintendent:

- An emotionally safe workplace
- Clear and reasonable expectations for work performance
- Honest, open communication
- The ability to operate their department without a lot of "micromanaging"
- An overall vision for the district and the department; some input on the overall direction in the district
- An open and "visible" supervisory process
- Feedback regarding performance
- Support and guidance when dealing with problem employees, parents, and situations

Key Point #1: Keep the needs of your senior-level cabinet members and principals in mind when you are considering your supervision strategies.

In your role as the superintendent you have considerable control over the strategies to meet these and other needs of your administrative staff. Let's look at some ideas and strategies that may help you within each of these areas.

An emotionally safe workplace: Employees have a right to work in settings where they feel safe from attacks and unreasonable distress. You need to set the tone and develop structures for this to occur. Many superintendents forget this important responsibility and allow the pressure they are facing in the district to impact the work conditions for their supervisory staff.

Keep these strategies in mind as you work to set a positive emotional tone in the workplace:

- **Set and follow through on group behavior norms:** At the beginning of the year, take some time to talk with your staff about what they need to feel emotionally safe in the workplace. Their needs will become the "norms of behavior" that will guide the operation of your supervisory staff in meetings and in their day-to-day operations. Norms we have implemented ourselves or seen implemented by superintendent/administrative teams in the past include the following:

  o   Team members will assume that everyone on our team brings their best intentions to work and meetings.
  o   As new ideas are presented regarding our work, members will listen to the entire idea before making comments in favor of or in opposition to the idea.
  o   Members of the administrative team will not discuss rumors outside of the team meeting; when rumors are heard, they will be discussed at team meetings.
  o   We will listen to all ideas before coming to a final decision when dealing with a problem.
  o   Team members will not raise their voices during emotional discussions.
  o   Administrative team members will not form voting blocks or coalitions to influence a particular decision.
  o   Matters discussed in administrative cabinet will not be shared outside of the group unless agreed upon by all members of the team.

These and other norms set the stage for the emotional safety of executive level staff members. As the superintendent it is your job to ensure that the group follows them even when they get off task or distracted. Here are some strategies we have used over the years to improve meeting behavior:

- **Develop your staff:** Take the time to develop your staff in relation to effective meeting behavior. Focus on a few key behaviors, introduce them to the administrators, then practice them on a regular basis. Your follow-up can be instrumental in making meetings productive and engaging opportunities to work together.

- **Meeting agendas and needs set in advance:** In some districts administrative staff is taken off guard and placed in a negative situation if they are required to answer questions when they don't have needed information at their disposal. When setting up meeting agendas, be sure to let everyone know the agenda topics and the information that will be needed for the meeting. By doing this you avoid catching them off guard, or unprepared. Remember, you want your administrators to be able to answer questions or provide information. Why would you call them together to embarrass them or put them on the spot? Model the kinds of behaviors you want them to use with their staff.

- **Phone messages:** When leaving phone messages for staff members, be sure to give them a general idea of what you want to talk with them about. Many subordinates fear a general message that offers little for the employee besides the fact that you want to talk with them. Many times superintendents are reluctant to leave a detailed message out of fear that someone else may pick up the message and talk about it. Make sure your administrative team members have confidential, password-protected voice mail systems. When you leave a more detailed message, not only does it lower the anxiety level of the person receiving it, but it also allows this person to spend the time you are waiting for their call to be returned to actually find the answer to your question or questions. This will be a real time saver for both of you.

- **Develop a process for handling concerns or negative situations:** Superintendents who develop and share with their administrators a process for handling problems or negative situations help these employees know what to expect when problems occur. Those superintendents who are reactionary and unpredictable set a negative work tone and can cause fear and resentment with their administrative team members. Figure 6.1 illustrates a process we have seen several superintendents use to make problem solving more predictable.

Key Point #2: An emotionally safe workplace does not preclude you from talking about difficult issues. It does require that you put in place stable policies and practices for your employees.

Figure 6.1 Sample Problem-Solving Process Guide

Problem-Solving Process for Achievement Valley Public Schools
Step 1: Gather data/ask nonjudgmental questions to thoroughly understand the problem.
Step 2: Talk through why the situation or problem is detrimental to the district.
Step 3: Brainstorm ideas and strategies to help eliminate the problem or bring it under control.
Step 4: Determine the implementation steps needed in order to begin to address the problem.
Step 5: Identify when the strategies will begin and who will be involved in the implementation of the strategies.
Step 6: Determine what data will be gathered and what conditions will constitute successful resolution of the problem.

- **Share your concerns about a person only with that person and in private:** This may be obvious, but we have seen new superintendents who have had real problems with this point. We have seen superintendents who talk about the administrative team members who are not present at a meeting in a negative manner. This kind of behavior can cause those who are present to wonder what is said about them when they are not present at a meeting. In the end, everyone loses when your integrity as their superintendent is undermined by talking about people rather than talking with them about situations or concerns.

Because the position of superintendent can be a lonely position, it is tempting to involve other administrators in employee situations. This type of behavior sets up a negative situation. Another undermining behavior we have seen is when superintendents confront administrative staff members in front of other administrators at cabinet or administrative meetings. When this has happened, both the administrator confronted and the others witnessing the confrontation have felt very uncomfortable. The tone in the room was very negative. Always deal with confrontations in private even if you have to schedule another meeting to take care of the problems.

- **If an employee causes a problem, but is supervised by a member of your administrative team, be sure to work with that administrator before talking to the problem employee.** Work together with your administrator to support him/her as they work through the issue with this employee. Nobody likes it when their superintendent gets too directly involved in business they are supposed to handle.
- **Find ways to help administrative team members work together to solve problem.** Identify the connections between departments when looking at problems. Help your administrators see how problems are related. If they can see how they can work together, it will help them develop positive working relationships. When team members begin to see the connections between each other and how they can access each other's strengths, they build interdependency. In interdependent relationships team members understand how to work together when needed and work alone as necessary.

Clear and reasonable expectations for work performance: When working with district level directors and supervisors, be clear in setting expectations for job performance with them. People at the administrative or department head level want a balance between autonomy (the ability to operate their department) and direction (information from you about what is required of them). By working with them and providing clear expectations, then letting them operate their department with your support, you set up an environment for positive results.

Honest, open communication: As the new superintendent, people will expect that you are open and honest with them while operating in a tactful manner. Be sure to provide your executive level staff members with the information they need to successfully operate their departments while letting them see the big picture of how their efforts benefit the entire organization and community. This information may take some thinking on your part because there is a balance between clear information and becoming reactionary and addressing every situation as a crisis. Sort through the sea of information that comes your way each day, think about what parts of it your executive staff needs in order to stay well informed, then try to provide them with clear and emotionally balanced information. If a board member has complained about their department, sort through the message and provide them with the information in a calm and forthright manner. Talk through your perceptions and work together to develop a plan to react to the message.

The ability to operate their department: People know that you are the leader of the district but they still want to be the leader of their own departments. Work with your executive staff members to show them you value their department and their leadership. Allow them the room to operate their department in light of district goals and objectives. When you disagree with an executive level staff member, talk with him or her in private. Allow the staff member to share his or her perspective about the situation, share your concern, and then come together on a plan that will move the department forward. Finding the proper balance between being totally hands-off and actually running the department takes thought and focus, but in the end you will do yourself and your staff members a favor by working to reach this balance between support and taking over the operation of their departments.

> **Key Point #3:** Even though you may be tempted to "get involved" in the operation of the various departments and schools under your indirect supervision, be sure to work through your directors and principals to keep them "in charge." In the long-term this will ensure a smoother operation and let you focus on more global, systemwide issues.

An overall vision for the district and the department: As the leader of the school district, one of your responsibilities is to develop an overall vision for it along with the school board. As you gather data and talk to school community members, keep your executive level staff members in the loop about what you are learning and how you might decide to use it. Involve them in reacting to the initial drafts of your vision for the district; allow them to help you shape and refine this vision. In the end your trust in their ideas allows them to feel they part of the process while also helping them to more clearly understand the direction and the specifics of the mission.

An open and "visible" supervisory process: In the honeymoon period of your superintendency, explore options regarding the supervision process. Discuss your ideas and let your executive-level staff members share their ideas. Even though you will be very busy you will find your time well spent discussing this important part of the process. Your supervisory process also says a lot about your relationships with your executive-level staff members. If you have a growing concern about their performance or department, start to talk about it in its intial stages if possible. If you wait and "spring" something negative on a staff member, they get the message that you are playing "gotcha" and will react accordingly. If you are open and honest and have a visible supervisory process, people will begin to know that you are open and honest in other areas of your superintendency. You set a good tone and will get the commitment and "buy in" from people when you operate an open and visible process.

Feedback regarding performance: In his book, *Primal Leadership*, author Daniel Goleman (2004) points out the importance of feedback. People want feedback. In the absence of feedback people will either think they are doing well and continue to move down their present path, or continually wonder how they are doing and operate in the dark. When you provide verbal and written comments, you give people the critical information they need in order to understand how they are doing and keep on track or make course adjustments to get themselves back on track. Good superintendents provide specific, focused, and sincere feedback regularly to their staff members.

> **Key Point #4:** When supervising employees, keep their need for feedback in mind. Be sure to provide both positive and refinement feedback to help them continue to grow in their roles.

Support and guidance when dealing with problem employees, parents, and situations: As the superintendent you have a balcony view of the entire operation of the district. You also have a somewhat neutral position in many incidents that happen in the district because you are not directly involved in all of the minute details of departmental operation. Since you are not emotionally involved in many situations, you can come in with a calm and objective viewpoint. Use this unique perspective to provide direction and guidance to executive level staff members when they are dealing with problems or difficult people. Since they can become immersed in the emotions of a situation, you can help them see an issue from another perspective. Let them know you will try to look at an issue objectively and guide them through a plan to address it and get the department back on track. By stating that your intention is to help them work through the issue, you can then attack it by lowering the emotions attached to the issue and begin to view it objectively. Even though some executive level staff members will want you to "take their side" on an issue, most will come to appreciate the fact that you are helping them work out the best overall solution by providing guidance and helping them to see all perspectives related to a problem.

Getting the Most From Your Staff Members

Most people want to do well in their positions. As their superintendents you set the stage for their success. Keep the following in mind as you work to get the most from your staff members:

- **People like to know you are interested in their success:** Communicate sincerely that you are interested in the success of your staff. People like to know that you care about them. If you are sincere, they will work hard to perform.
- **Work with staff members to set clear, attainable goals:** The key here is to work with people rather than just tell others what to do.

Everyone likes some input into their work. Work with staff to evaluate their progress as they implement the goals you have jointly set.

- **Be clear in your expectations:** Clarity can go a long way to help establish and maintain a successful employer-employee relationship. Don't "beat around the bush" when setting work expectations. If you are clear, your staff will understand that their work is important and needs to be taken seriously.
- **Treat executive staff members as individuals but also as part of a team:** Avoid singling out members for mistakes or "pitting" one member against another for attention. Try to help staff members work together when needed but also be able to move their divisions forward in their own unique ways.
- **Offer praise and incentives:** People will work hard for a thank you or for some small, seemingly insignificant incentive. We know of one superintendent who really got a lot out of his employees by covering their job for a day when they had completed something significant. The "award" didn't cost much, but it motivated people and also helped him establish and maintain his credibility by covering staff member duties.

SUPERVISION STRATEGIES FOR DIRECTORS AND DEPARTMENT/DIVISIONAL ADMINISTRATORS

As the district superintendent you are responsible for a diverse group of directors and administrators. You will not have the expertise in each individual area to provide direct guidance and instruction. You will quickly need to assess each of your departments to determine its level of operation and how much direct supervision you will need to provide in order to help the department do its best. How do you gather this kind of information? Here are some of the strategies employed by successful superintendents:

- Meet with the administrator/director to talk about the level of operation and the needs of the department.
- Meet individually with employees within each division of the school district to find out their perceptions of its operation. A form listing possible questions is included in Figure 6.2.
- Meet in small focus groups with employees to gain their perceptions of the division and its operation. A form to conduct these focus groups is in Figure 6.3.
- Gain feedback from the clients of the particular division. For the custodial/maintenance department, contact teachers, administrators, groups renting the building, and so on. For the transportation department, contact parents, students, and specific administrators at school sites. For sample feedback questions, see

Figure 6.4. With these groups you can conduct individual discussions, focus groups, or surveys.

- Observe the various departments/divisions within your school district. As you watch these divisions in action, take notes and jot down what you are seeing and questions you have for employees and the directors/administrators in these divisions.

Figure 6.2   Department/Division Employee Interview Feedback Form

Use this form to assist you as you conduct individual conferences with employees to assess the effectiveness of departments/divisions in the school district. Ask the questions as they are listed. Stop, listen, and let the employee talk openly in response to the questions. Be careful not to lead the employee(s) in a particular direction.

How do you think the department/division operates in general? Provide specific examples that led you to your perceptions.

_____

_____

_____

In what areas does the department/division do a good job? Share specific examples.

_____

_____

_____

What needs to be improved in the department/division? How would you suggest that we move forward in making these improvements?

_____

_____

_____

What other comments/suggestions do you have in relation to this department/division?

_____

_____

_____

Figure 6.3 Department/Division Employee Focus Group Feedback Form

Use this form to assist you as you conduct small group employee focus groups to assess the effectiveness of departments/divisions in the school district. Ask the questions as they are listed. Stop, listen, and let the employee/employees talk openly in response to the questions. Be careful not to lead the employee(s) in a particular direction.

What are your general perceptions of the department/division?

_____

_____

_____

In what areas does the department/division do a *good* job?

_____

_____

_____

In what areas does the department/division do *less than* a good job?

_____

_____

What needs to be improved in the department/division?

_____

_____

_____

In what areas do you have comments that we have not yet discussed?

_____

_____

_____

Figure 6.4   Department/Division Client/Customer Feedback Form

Use this form to assist you as you gather the perceptions of the department/division in relation to how well it meets client expectations for the delivery of products or services.

Are you an internal or external customer or client of the department/division?

_____

_____

_____

Describe the nature of your "business" with this department/division?

_____

_____

_____

In relation to your expectations for service, how well has the department/division met your expectations? Describe in detail.

_____

_____

What are the strengths or positive attributes of this department/division?

_____

_____

_____

What are the areas that need improvement in this department/division?

_____

_____

_____

What other comments do you have about this department/division?

_____

_____

_____

Key Point #5: Use a variety of data sources when gathering information to evaluate the performance of divisions or departments. This will help you make sure that you get a balanced look at these divisions or departments and provide guidance to help improve their operation.

Using the data you have gathered put together a profile/performance baseline for each division/department. Rate each based on its prescribed function. Use your data as the basis of discussions and ultimate goal-setting processes in the future. Figure 6.5 (pp. 130–131) is an example of a generic summative evaluation form that can be used to combine the results of your data gathering efforts related to department or division operations. You can add in specifics based on each department's unique contribution to the overall effectiveness of the school district.

EVALUATING DEPARTMENT HEADS, ASSISTANT SUPERINTENDENTS, AND DIRECTORS

You face a complex task as the new superintendent: how to evaluate your directors and administrators. These people represent a very diverse and varied group of employees. Each director may think and process differently based on the "content" of the field that he or she supervises. Keep the following in mind as you begin to think about how to supervise this group:

- **The skills needed to work in each particular field:** Each division or department in your school district requires a slightly different skill set in order to be success. In the transportation department for example, the director may need to be able to work with complex schedules and motivate a mixed group of male and female drivers. A special education director may need to be able to remember a large amount of information plus be able to calm down potentially hostile situations. The skill sets of your directors of these departments/divisions will require slightly different supervision behaviors from you as the superintendent. For some directors you may need to be more direct; for others you will need to be subtler in your approach to supervision.
- **The type of personality typically attracted to each field:** This element is related to the first element in some manner but is important enough that it needs to be mentioned as a separate category. Certain departments may attract certain personality types. A custodial director may have worked his way up from the labor force and may not need a lot of conversation in relation to her evaluation, while the community relations director may have a

Figure 6.5 Sample Department/Division Summative Evaluation Form

---

Program/Departmental Evaluation

Department/program: _____

Data gathering period—dates/times: _____

Directions: For each area indicate a number that best describes the level of performance of the department/division.

3 – Department/division is exceeding expectations in this area.

2 – Department/division is meeting expectations in this area.

1 – Department/division is not meeting expectations in this area.

1. Delivery of Service/Product, Promotes Itself to Clients

1a. ☐ Department/division has clear understanding of the product/service it is designed to deliver.

1b. ☐ Department/division delivers product service in timely manner.

1c. ☐ Department/division delivers product service in attractive manner.

1d. ☐ Department/division delivers product service in an efficient manner.

1e. ☐ Department/division promotes itself to internal clients.

1f. ☐ Department/division promotes itself to external clients.

Comments:

2. Employee Attitudes

2a. ☐ Department/division promotes a clear mission for its service and responsibilities to all employees.

2b. ☐ Employees understand mission and vision of organization and can articulate the mission and vision.

2c. ☐ Employees demonstrate the mission and vision of the department/division.

2d. ☐ Employees model good communication skills both internally with each other and externally with clients.

2e. ☐ Division/department has established process for conflict resolution and problem solving.

| **Comments:** |
| |

Customer Service

3a. ☐ Employees of the department/division understand and exhibit good customer service skills.

3b. ☐ The department regularly gathers information about the perceptions of its customer service.

3c. ☐ The department has a process for improving customer service.

3d. ☐ Employees are rewarded for providing good customer service.

3e ☐ Employees show professionalism when dealing with customers.

| **Comments:** |
| |

Professional Development, Care for Employees, Care for Equipment, etc.

4a. ☐ Regular training and staff development is offered by the department.

4b. ☐ Staff actively participate in staff development opportunities.

4c. ☐ Department employees understand how to operate and care for major equipment that they use on the job.

4d. ☐ Departmental equipment is well-maintained and serviced, equipment is current and up to date.

4e. ☐ An equipment replacement/maintenance schedule is in place and implemented.

4f. ☐ Staff members know how to access employee services, supervisors take an interest in the well-being of their employees.

| **Comments:** |
| |

_____   _____

Signatures (Superintendent/department director)   Date

more verbal personality and needs to have a more verbal supervision process. How does a new superintendent quickly figure out the supervision needs of her directors? One way is to talk with them and observe them in action. Another is to just ask them what their supervision needs are; many people will tell you exactly what they need if you just ask.

- **Possible motivations that each person could have and want to accomplish:** From our observations over the years, department directors can have issues that impact their supervision needs. One situation we observed recently involved a director who wanted to test the resolve of a recently appointed superintendent. This new superintendent was appointed over a colleague of the director. The superintendent had to take this situation into account as he worked with her in the supervision process. He found that she needed a more direct approach in working with her to set her annual goals than other directors since she doubted his abilities as a superintendent because of the situation with her friend who did not get the job. This superintendent also had to be more direct with her when she questioned some of his decisions. (Yes, believe it or not, some members of your administrative team may actually question your decisions!)

- **The hierarchy or operation represented by each head of the departments/divisions:** In some districts certain departments historically have had a more prestigious or greater position on the district hierarchy. As a new superintendent you need to take these histories into account and do what is necessary in order to elevate all departments to an appropriate level. For example, in one district we observed, the director of instruction was evaluated by analyzing her goals, while the custodial/maintenance department director wasn't formally evaluated. This practice led to the maintenance director feeling that his department wasn't as important as the instructional department. Over time the condition of the buildings was going downhill. Tom, a superintendent new to the school district, found this out as he assessed the district operations and quickly worked with the director of maintenance to develop a set of yearly goals that would serve as his evaluation. This practice helped to elevate the status of the custodial/maintenance department and improve its level of operation. In other cases, department heads who have not had to be subject to accountability measures or standards may think that they are privileged or have favor with the superintendent. You will need to assess this kind of situation and respond accordingly. Sit down with the department head and explain why you need to hold him accountable just like the other departments in the district. We have seen situations where a department head has tried to cause trouble for a new superintendent, so be careful as you move forward to increase accountability. Some of these department heads may have powerful ties or connections within the community and you'll need to recognize these as you make decisions about increasing their level of accountability.

- **Traditional histories of the various groups and how they work together:** The relationship histories of the directors of the departments in the school district can have an impact on the supervision process. If different departments have been cooperative and implemented joint goals together over the years, you may be able to involve the directors in setting common improvement plans. If the departments are competitive and don't get along, you may need to avoid putting strategies in place that would cause group members to develop hostile relationships and competitions because they are required to work together. It may take some time before these groups could actually begin to work on common goals and projects and be able to be evaluated on the progress of multiple goals. As the superintendent you will need to build the interdependent relationships of these groups before asking them to work together.

- **Each director's perception of and attitude toward supervision:** Some people view supervision as a negative process where they are watched and rated. These people may need an evaluation process that includes them in setting some of the parameters of the evaluation. Others may not see supervision as a big deal and might be more willing to be supervised and welcome ideas and suggestions for growth. Assess your directors' attitudes toward supervision by watching them in supervisory settings and by asking for their perceptions of past experiences. You may need to develop a trusting relationship with them before they will "warm up" to your feedback. Don't avoid contact and evaluative interactions with them while you are developing your relationship. Even though they might not welcome your feedback, you will still need to evaluate their performance while you are working to build their trust in your leadership.

GOAL SETTING

In today's educational organizations, goal setting has become very popular. While setting and reaching goals can be motivating for a lot of those in director positions, it can also be a way for people to lower their performance and commitment to the success of the district. In workshops we have conducted in the past regarding goal setting, we have shared the following considerations:

- Goals should be attainable but cause the person setting them to reach a little in order to accomplish them.
- Goals need to be measurable and as specific as possible.

- Employee evaluation goals are normally long-term in nature (usually one or two academic years), involve regular check-ups, and include assessment strategies that ensure their periodic monitoring.
- For employees to be involved in their own goal setting, they should be at least proficient in the basic tasks required for their job success. If they are below the district standards for an area or areas, the supervisor can assist in or set their goals. Addressing the deficiencies should become the basis for the goals that are established for the supervision process.

Key Point #6: Goal setting can be a highly effective and motivating way to implement director evaluation. Keep in mind that before anyone is allowed to participate in goal setting, that person should be meeting district standards for his or her job area.

While each director may need a slightly different process for goal setting, there are some common elements that should be in place for people to be successful in the process. The forms in Figures 6.6 and 6.7 can be used by you and your directors in the goal setting and implementation process.

Figure 6.6   Director Goal Setting Worksheet

Use this worksheet as way to focus your efforts for setting yearly goals that can help move your department forward and positively contribute to the school district.

1.   In what general areas do you feel you or your department need to improve or grow?

2.   What data or information did you use to make your determination in question 1?

3.   Within the general areas specified in question 1, what specific goals or focus areas do you think will best benefit you and your department in the next 12 months?

4.   For each specific area in question 3, write a goal statement. Be sure your goal statement is specific, measurable, attainable, and fits into the parameters of the fiscal year.

Figure 6.7   Director Goal Implementation and Assessment Sheet

Use this form to list your goals, the sub-goal activities that will be needed to ensure successful completion of the goals, and how you will assess the goal to look for progress and areas needing refinement.

Name: _____

Department: _____

Department Needs: _____

_____

_____

Assessments and Data Used to Determine Department Needs: _____

_____

_____

General Goals for the Year: _____

_____

_____

Goal Area	Resources Needed to Attain Goal	Goal Implementation Timeline	Schedule of Meetings to Monitor Goal	Indicators of Success

Summary of Progress for the Year/Possible Goals for Next Year: _____

_____

_____

_____

SUMMARY

One of the challenges you will face as a new superintendent is your responsibility in evaluating a wider variety of staff members than you did as a principal. Some of these employees perform jobs that you may know very little about. For some new superintendents this can be a daunting responsibility, while for others it all comes together. As you move forward on this important task, think about the following questions:

- How can I find out about the effectiveness of the various departments in my district?
- How does employee goal setting work and what strategies can I use to implement it in my district?
- What specialized skills and abilities do I need to take into account when supervising principals and directors?

Employee supervision can be one of the most challenging, yet rewarding, parts of your job as a superintendent. By working with your staff in an open supervision environment, you will make your job easier and be clearer in your expectations for the leadership performance of your principals and directors.

Instructional leadership is an important but often neglected part of the job of a superintendent. In the next chapter, What About the Students? Instructional Leadership and Dealing With Federal Programs, we'll take a look at some powerful instructional leadership strategies you can employ as a superintendent. The aspect of instructional leadership is one reason why many of us got into education in the first place. Enjoy the chapter and find several ideas you can use as you begin your superintendency.

7

What About the Students?

Instructional Leadership and Dealing With Federal Programs

*One hundred years from now, it will not matter what
my bank account was, how big my house was, or what
kind of car I drove. But the world may be a little better,
because I was important in the life of a child.*
—Forest Witcraft

Many of us get involved in education in order to make a difference in the success and achievement of students. The role of the superintendent of schools can be complex and overwhelming. It is easy to lose sight of the reason we got into this business in the first place: to help students. Keeping your focus on student achievement while managing all of the other responsibilities of a school superintendent can be challenging.

ABOUT THIS CHAPTER

In this chapter the aspects of instructional leadership and the influences of federal programs will be highlighted. It may seem like these two topics are not related, but they do fit together. Superintendents tend to be pulled in a variety of directions but they still need to find a way to enable their district to focus on the success of the students. The following areas will be addressed in this chapter:

- The instructional leadership role of school superintendents; techniques and strategies to have a positive impact on student achievement as a superintendent
- Leading a school district in light of the No Child Left Behind Act and increased accountability
- The impact of special education legislation and programming

In many districts the instructional aspects of its operation have been led by assistants and directors. Even though the role of the superintendency has gravitated toward leadership and management of the entire operation, instructional leadership is crucial to your success. How can an effective superintendent be an instructional leader while tending to the managerial aspects of a district? What kinds of leadership behaviors hold promise to positively impact the achievement of students?

INSTRUCTIONAL LEADERSHIP

Lars Bork (1993) proposes a set of leadership behaviors that seem to positively impact student achievement. In his article he states:

> Improving education, however, requires district leadership. Research studies indicate that superintendents who serve as instructional leaders contribute to the instructional effectiveness of their school districts. (Bork, 1993, p. 249)

Later in his article he proposes five major areas where superintendents can positively impact student achievement in their districts based on research focused on Instructionally Effective School Districts (IESD). Those areas include the following:

1. Staff selection and recruitment
2. Principal supervision and evaluation
3. Establishing clear instructional and curricular goals
4. Maintaining and monitoring instructional and curricular focus
5. Financial planning for instruction (Bork, 1993, p. 252)

Let's take a brief look at each of these areas and strategies you should consider as you work to improve the student achievement in your district.

Key Point #1: Your role as an instructional leader should be prominent as the superintendent. Be sure to think about the ways you could model and provide influence on the instructional mission of the school district.

Staff recruitment and selection: One area where a superintendent can have a positive impact on student achievement is the selection and recruitment of staff members. This role includes not only staff members at the district level but also building level instructional staff. This may be easy if you are the superintendent of a small, rural district, but how is it possible in a large or even medium-sized district? In this section we discuss strategies that we, along with our colleagues, have used over the years to stay involved in the selection and recruitment process. In Figure 7.1, an outline we use in helping schools develop selection and recruitment processes is presented, which you can modify for your own use.

Figure 7.1   An Outline for Designing a Recruitment/Selection Process

Recruitment and Selection of Staff

Recruiting and selecting effective staff is one of the most important processes to ensure school operations support the school's purpose. The recruitment and selection process requires planning and real thought into answering the questions: What are we looking for? Where are we going to look? How are we going to select the best candidate?

The following ten-step process will help you decide how to answer these questions.

1. **Write a role description for each staff role.** To do this well you must articulate the major work areas (classroom teaching, staff team work, parent relations, etc.), goals, and behavioral expectations/competencies for each role. Be sure to be as concrete as possible and include any "extracurricular" duties (e.g., committee assignment, student groups, sport team supervision) generally expected of the position.

2. **Identify required and desired qualifications and characteristics.** Pull directly from your role description. A few general categories to consider include: subject matter knowledge; instructional and assessment practices; classroom management skills; knowledge of child development; awareness of typical issues facing the school's student body, such as teamwork and cooperation, goal-setting, overcoming obstacles, and interpersonal influence skills.

(Continued)

Figure 7.1 (Continued)

3. **Identify potential sources of staff.** Use your existing personal and professional networks heavily, and build on any new relationships quickly to create new recruiting sources.

4. **Promote your school.** The key to hiring the best candidates is to promote your school district so that the best-matched candidates are more likely to accept positions. Be sure to share a copy of the mission and relevant materials with all candidates, share student and parent testimonials, and give finalists tours of the school and let them observe classes.

5. **Recruit.** Be sure that your recruitment effort is multi-pronged, reaching out to several pools of potential candidates.

6. **Determine how you will screen candidates.** Education and experience cited can be checked through references. Content knowledge may be checked through testing, references, and indicators of educational achievement; interviews typically are not an effective way to check content knowledge unless extensive time is available. Competencies or behavioral characteristics may best be screened through interviews or on-the-job observation (if possible). Consider any legal and regulatory restrictions on hiring that apply in your state.

7. **Prepare materials and organize assistance.** Compile documents (such as the resume, cover letter, references, assessments from classroom observations, etc.) into a profile to be reviewed before interviewing the candidate. Create or adopt some type of rating system that will allow you to assess and compare each candidate objectively. Determine who is involved in the selection process—your school would probably be well served by using a review panel composed of members who each bring different perspectives to the table.

8. **Make initial selections.** Once you have assembled the appropriate materials and assessed the individual candidates, you will be ready to make your initial selection decisions. Keep in mind that if you want your teachers to work as a team you will need to consider how each hire will contribute as a team member.

9. **Notify all candidates of outcomes.** Communicate offers in person by phone (with follow-up written offers). Clarify the role for which you are offering a job, compensation/benefits (see later section), and timing of the job (When does it start? Is it a 10- or 12-month schedule? and so on). Consider communicating rejections to borderline candidates by phone (with follow-up letter) as soon as possible. Let all other unsuccessful candidates know your decision in writing, and express your thanks for their trouble; letters need not be customized, just polite.

10. **Draw up the contract.** In general some topics you may want to incorporate into a contract include professional expectations and standards, duration of contract, work year, work day, salary, benefits, evaluation, days allotted for illness and personal needs, leaves of absence, termination stipulations, and grievance procedures.

Practical ideas for superintendents to participate in the selection/recruitment process of instructional staff include the following:

- Participate in the design of the criteria used for selection of instructional staff.
- Build in selection instrumentation that requires district office participation in the process; meet with district level staff to review recent hires and their match to selection standards.
- Assist principals and school-level selection teams with designing selection criteria.
- Sit in on interviews as an active participant.
- Perform reference checks.
- Require all instructional staff to "meet" the superintendent.
- Participate in the development of the induction plan for the new employee.

Key Point #2: The selection and recruitment of instructional staff can be one of the most important decisions you make as the school district's instructional leader. Make sure you have a role in this process in your district.

Principal supervision and evaluation: We talked about the supervision and evaluation of principals in Chapter 6, but this crucial area of superintendent leadership cannot be over emphasized.

Establishing clear instructional and curricular goals: Facilitating the process for the district-level goals and objectives to be aligned with building-level goals is crucial to the instructional leadership role of the superintendent. Some of our colleagues in the past have worked with the board to set a number of district-level goals and then required the buildings to adopt goals aligned with them, while other school districts ask buildings to develop student achievement-based goals then use those to set the district goals. We have seen both processes be successful if the district and the schools are focused on student achievement and work together for the common good of students. Keep the following in mind when establishing clear instructional and curricular goals:

- Keep the number of goals manageable; we have found that three to four well designed and meaningful goals is about the maximum number that can be managed at a time.
- Make sure the goals have a balance between being specific and very general; you should be able to visualize what the organization will look like once the goal is attained.

- Make sure the goal can be measured and assessed; avoid broad and hard to quantify goals.
- Write goals that start and end. You may need to take a larger effort, break it into parts, and successfully complete one part before moving onto the next. People benefit from small, measurable successes.
- Work to design goals that have specific actions associated with them rather than goals that are philosophical in nature; people can relate to action.

Key Point #3: Your support and supervision of principals can have a positive impact on the level of student success and achievement in your district. Keep student learning at the forefront of your conversations and discussions related to principals and building operations.

Maintaining and monitoring an instructional and curricular focus: Work with your administrators to design effective strategies to monitor goals throughout the year. Some methods superintendents have used in this area are as follows:

- Regular goal reports that include data related to student achievement
- Focused site visits conducted by the superintendent to observe student achievement efforts
- Curriculum maps submitted by staff illustrating acquisition of curricular objectives by students
- Focus groups or students that can be interviewed by the superintendent in relation to student achievement efforts
- Student exit outcome performances that the superintendent can attend where students are demonstrating achievement gains
- Faculty focus groups the superintendent can meet with to discuss student achievement gains and challenges related to school and district goals

Financial planning for instruction: As simple as it may seem that the majority of funding should be dedicated to student learning in a district, it is surprising how easy it is to lose sight of this principle when managing the budget. It is far too simple to say "just do it" in relation to making sure that the majority of funding is dedicated to raising student achievement in a school district. Here are some ideas we have seen used in the past by effective superintendents:

- The formation of a district spending advisory committee. This committee looks at budgets and budget requests to see how each fits into the aspect of student achievement improvement.

- Requiring school buildings and departments to include detailed descriptions that show how their budget priorities impact student learning.
- Asking the major departments in a school district to present their major budget priorities and how they relate to student achievement in a joint department meeting.
- Creating a budget development form that requires departments and buildings to address questions related to their spending and student achievement improvement.
- Offering a chance for mini-grants to be used for innovative instructional improvement ideas and initiatives.
- Offering sites and departments the freedom to restructure their school around student achievement initiatives; open staffing and instructional support budgets up to allow buildings flexibility.

Key Point #4: The phrase "putting your money where your mouth is" applies to your budgeting practices as they relate to student learning. Get in the habit of asking yourself "How does this area we are considering spending money on impact student learning?" every time you consider a budgetary item. This practice will help you maintain your focus on students and their learning.

NO CHILD LEFT BEHIND ACT

In 2002 President George W. Bush signed the Elementary and Secondary Education Act (ESEA), commonly known as the No Child Left Behind Act (NCLB). The act was designed to increase the federal role in education. The act was also designed to increase educational accountability and set "achievement bars" for schools to use in measuring the growth of their students. The law required states to set progress standards and develop assessments to measure these standards. The No Child Left Behind Act had profound impacts on public education in the United States.

At the time this book was written Congress was in the process of the reauthorization process of ESEA (NCLB). Rather than provide details of the original law, we chose to provide you with strategies to deal with NCLB in whatever final form that emerges from Congress. Here are ideas and strategies to use to learn about the law and the implications for your district:

- Strategies to become knowledgeable about NCLB
  - Contact your state AASA affiliate: They will have up-to-date knowledge about the law and its implications.

- ○ Contact your state department of education: Since the new version of NCLB will probably be based on state assessments and achievement standards to some extent, your state department of education should have brochures and informational meetings scheduled in your region to help you understand the new refinements to the law.
  - ○ Go to the U.S. Department of Education Web site at http://www.ed.gov: This site will feature many resources that can help you understand the law and its implications.

- Strategies to help the district be successful in the areas impacted by NCLB

  - ○ Work with your instructional staff to ensure there are school improvement plans in place that address the requirements of NCLB.
  - ○ Make sure that your district assessment data is disaggregated based on the major student population groups present in your district.
  - ○ Know the standards that are used to identify students and poorly performing schools (currently called "not making Adequate Yearly Progress [AYP]"). Make sure you know which of your schools is either close to not achieving appropriately or have already been identified as performing poorly. Be sure to work with the staff at these schools to address the situation.
  - ○ Make sure each school has the data to understand what it will take to achieve AYP.
  - ○ Make sure each teacher has the data required to know where each of their students is currently performing.
  - ○ Understand the "penalties" associated with poor academic performance; be ready to deal with the negative aspects of the penalties (for example, loss of a portion of Title I funding due to requirements for student tutoring or school transfer options).
  - ○ Produce informational brochures outlining the major aspects of the NCLB law, how the district is working hard to improve student achievement, and parental rights under the law. Your local AASA affiliate should have examples for you to use in developing you own brochure.
  - ○ Set aside budget money to address the problems that will have the most impact on your district in meeting the standards of the new NCLB legislation. In the past, some districts found it beneficial to focus their efforts on groups experiencing gaps in achievement in order to be successful in improving overall student achievement.

SPECIAL EDUCATION

Another broad area of programming that has profound impacts on school districts is the area of special education. In most districts, a special education director is employed to assist with the districtwide management of special education programs. This special education director is someone you will need to quickly get to know. He or she can be one person that helps keep the district out of trouble.

Below are some of the foundations of special education that may help you as you work with your special education director to implement programs in your district:

- **Least restrictive environment:** This term essentially means that the student should be educated in an environment that best provides for his or her needs while also providing them with as "normal" a classroom experience as possible. The least restrictive environment is based on the input of a student study team and the parents of the student.
- **Student study process:** When a child is being considered for possible placement in a special education program a multidisciplinary team of professionals needs to assess the student using a variety of instruments or observations. The results of this assessment are discussed at a study team meeting or a staffing.
- **Student staffing:** Although this process has different names in several states, the process is guided by federal legislation and similar from state-to-state. The multidisciplinary team members meet with the parents to discuss the results of the various assessments and whether or not the student requires formal intervention to address the disability that is negatively impacting the student's academic achievement. A program of learning is developed using input from the parents, the classroom teacher, and the multidisciplinary team members. This program of learning is normally written on a form that is called an Individual Education Plan. This Individual Education Plan or IEP is a binding contract between the student/parent and the school district for the implementation of the services the student needs to be successful related to his or her learning goals.
- **Periodic reviews:** Even though these also have different names in various states, each student in a special education program is required to have periodic reviews of his or her progress. The results of these reviews determine if the student will continue to receive special education or be placed back in the regular classroom.

Special education programs can be quite comprehensive in nature and expensive to operate. You may have some students served in your own district or some of your students may be served in another district. Even if students are served outside of your district, you are still responsible for their well being and education. Since special education is so important and a source of possible lawsuits, you will want to become knowledgeable about the specifics of your programs and unique issues as soon as possible. This will warrant a series of conversations with your special education director and staff members. Listed below are some details you will want to find out as a result of your meetings with these staff members.

Details to gather in conversations with special education staff members:

- What are the various disabilities present in the students that live within the district? What other disabilities exist in students served in district-sponsored programs?
- What has been the history of service provided by district special education programs? Have parents been satisfied with these services or have their been a lot of complaints regarding the special education services offered?
- What has been the relationship level between parents of special needs students and special education staff members? Have there been negative situations, arguments, or even lawsuits in relation to special education?
- What is the rate of success of special education programs in the district? Are students improving in their disability areas or are they staying the same?
- Where are the students being served? What are the classrooms and other facilities like that house special education students?
- What kinds of issues or negative situations has the special education department experienced over the years? Were the issues resolved? How were they resolved?
- How many students are coming to the school district from outside of the district to participate in district-sponsored programs? Does their tuition cover the cost of providing their services? How do they get to these programs?
- Does the district offer the right programs to meet student needs? How many students are being served on waivers because the district does not offer the programs designed to meet their needs?
- How is paperwork on special education programming and students being kept current in order to comply with state law? Does the district go through a periodic audit of its paperwork? If there are paperwork issues, what is the plan for addressing these issues as soon as possible?

- What outside agencies support the school district in implementing special education programming? How helpful are these agencies and what is the true cost of their services? How are their services "supervised" and evaluated by the school district?
- What is the board's perception and understanding of special education? What comments have board members made in the past to undermine the program? How has the board supported the program?
- What structures does the school district have in place to provide oversight and direction to the special education program? How are negative allegations investigated and the results communicated? How does the district provide information to the public about its special education programming and processes?

SUMMARY

In this chapter we provided an overview into ideas and strategies that can be used to enhance your instructional leadership skills as a superintendent. We have also briefly talked about two major federal programs and their influence on school districts and student learning. The topics touched on in this chapter are very complex, but hopefully we have provided you with a beginning point from which to launch your learning. As you review the content of this chapter, think about the following questions:

- How can superintendents provide instructional leadership in their districts?
- What attributes of a superintendent's leadership most positively impacts student learning?
- How do I find out how our special education department is functioning? What do I need to do in order to improve its function?

Instructional leadership is a journey, not a destination. Keep this in mind as you continue to work through the opportunities and the difficulties provided to you as the chief educational officer of your school district.

The old expression "The buck stops here" applies to you as the superintendent of schools. People at other levels of the school district can all say, "The final decision is not mine, you'll have to speak to the superintendent." Since the "buck" does stop with you, it is inevitable that you will have to learn how to deal with people who are upset or difficult. In Chapter 8, Dealing With Difficult People and Situations, you will learn strategies to help you with this task.

8

Dealing With Difficult People and Situations

When I hear somebody sigh, "Life is hard," I am always tempted to ask, "Compared to what?"

—Sydney J. Harris

As the leader of the school district, you are one of the most visible employees. A significant number of the people you interact with want you to make your decisions to favor their position or way of thinking. Some of these people have learned that becoming difficult will help them shape decisions in their favor. While many superintendents are able to work through these situations in a productive manner, others allow these difficult people to make their lives miserable or manipulate the decisions they are required to make. What makes the difference for successful superintendents?

ABOUT THIS CHAPTER

In this chapter we will examine the phenomenon of difficult people and strategies designed to help you deal with them in a productive manner.

As you read through this chapter, pay particular attention to the following:

- What's behind negative behavior
- Negative reinforcement and how it is often used
- Understanding others' perspectives
- Types of conflict you will face in the superintendency
- Strategies for dealing with difficult people
- Positive problem-solving strategies
- Conflict mediation
- Achieving positive interaction with the press

WHAT'S BEHIND ALL OF THIS NEGATIVE BEHAVIOR?

In our society people are facing increasing professional, personal, and economic pressure. Many of your constituents may come from homes where one parent is raising children solo or where both parents are working in order to provide a basic level of living. We are being threatened from unknown terrorists both inside and outside of the country. Jobs that were once secure can now be eliminated with little or no notice. Taxes are continually rising to meet increased government operational costs while citizens are continually reminded that their schools are in need of reform and restructuring. The list of pressures facing your school community members is endless.

All of these pressures work to keep people on edge and jumpy. Increased stress leaves many people ready to snap. For some, if one little thing goes wrong in their lives, they are on the attack. In many cases the negative behaviors you see in the parents and community members you interact with are not directly caused by anything major that you did; instead some little school district problem became the straw that broke the camel's back. The reactions that you will face as a superintendent don't always match the severity of the issues that you see as the school district leader.

Frames of Reference

There are many ideas about what makes some people difficult. We have found over the years that some of the issues we've encountered with difficult people involve how they think and came to their opinions. Their way of thinking seems to involve a pattern of behavior. A number of years ago we encountered the work of Thomas Kuhn in his book, *The Structure of Scientific Revolutions* (1962). This book outlined the process involved in major scientific discoveries that sometimes involve sudden shifts in thinking. The book also describes a process where people develop "frames of reference" that guide how they think and respond to situations.

The "frame of reference" model has helped us understand people's perspective as we have worked with them. Over the years we modified Kuhn's model to help explain how difficult people may have become difficult.

Frames of reference are related to difficult people and behavior:

- People have experiences where they see and hear information and experience ideas. As a result of these experiences they begin to draw conclusions about the world around them
- These conclusions get reinforced over time and they begin to form an initial frame of reference related to their experiences. These frames of reference start to guide their thinking and shape how they see the world.
- Their frame of reference becomes strong, and they become comfortable with their thought pattern; other thoughts become foreign or hard for them to accept; they become set in their ways

Establishing ways of thinking or frames of reference is a natural process and works both to our benefit and detriment. On the positive side, if we weren't able to develop patterns of thinking, we would have to re-learn a lot of the behaviors that we do seemingly without thinking each day. On the negative side, once people become comfortable with their way of thinking or frame of reference, it can be difficult for them to see another perspective or way of thinking. The investment they have in the frame of reference can cause them to "dig in" on issues when they conflict with how they see the world.

Looking at the second part of the model, we see how people's minds can become resistant to changing ideas and how some people eventually change their opinions on issues.

- People who have developed a solid frame of reference may encounter a new experience or new information.
- Because the new experience or information conflicts with their existing thought pattern, they resist considering the new information as valid. In order to preserve their old way of thinking, they bend or change the new information so that it fits their old or existing thought pattern. We may see this process as resistance to change but they may think they are just staying true to their thoughts and assumptions.

You may recognize this behavior as "excuse making" or resistance. The difficult or resistant person is normally trying to change the information to fit his or her thought patterns. As leaders sometimes we try to force our ideas on others or put pressure on them to conform to our way of thinking.

When we do this some people "dig in" and become even more resistant. We see this behavior as becoming more difficult or challenging our authority. As these people are continually exposed to the new ideas or thought patterns, their minds need to assimilate the new information and make it "fit." The next part of the model begins to address this condition.

- New thought formation or change requires forming a new thought pattern or different thinking than was required in the past.
- Once people begin to see that the new idea has merit they start to form a new frame of reference and their thinking can change. The new thought pattern or frame of reference now becomes more formed and permanent. It will be used to sort incoming information that this person receives over time. If he or she encounters new information of a new way of thinking, that new information will not fit the frame of reference and the reformation process of the frame or way of thinking will need to start over. Essentially, the reception of new information and the reforming of frames of reference is a constant process in our lives and the lives of those we work with. (Adapted from *The Structure of Scientific Revolutions*, Kuhn, 1962)

The real strength of this model involves understanding how frames of reference develop and how strongly held they can be by some people. This is important for you as a new superintendent because you will deal with many people that have formed definite ideas about a variety of topics. Some of these people will come to board meetings to share their opinions while others will meet with you privately for the same purpose. During these initial meetings it is crucial for you to listen and avoid disagreeing too soon with their points of view. If you set up an adversarial situation by disagreeing from the start of your interactions with others they might dig in on an issue and have a hard time working with you.

Obviously if you encounter someone who has an opinion that is detrimental to the dignity of others or violates one of your most closely held values, you may need to disagree with them. In these cases, you may need to stand your ground and make sure they know your "bottom line." In most situations you will be able to listen as they talk and try to figure out their perspective and how to begin to connect with them to impact their thought process.

Key Point #1: As a superintendent you deal with people who come from a variety of backgrounds and experiences. Many of them may bring issues from other experiences to their interactions with you. Try to consider the origins of negative behavior as you work with others.

NEGATIVE REINFORCEMENT

Taking a behaviorist's view (which many people can relate to from previous school or work experiences), negative or difficult behaviors may fit into the idea of negative reinforcement. In negative reinforcement, the sender of the negative message is counting on the fact that the receiver of the negative reinforcement or message dislikes it and will change his or her behavior in order to diminish or remove it. The negative person is banking on the fact that you, as the receiver, will want the negative behavior they are implementing to stop and you will do just about anything in order to make that happen. Some theorists debate the effectiveness of this idea, but we see it in operation all the time. For example, if you've recently visited a grocery store you may have witnessed this scene: A parent with little children is approaching the checkout lane when his children ask to buy some candy. The parent responds responsibly by saying "no." The children start to whine and cry until finally the negative behavior gets too great for the parent to handle and he gives in and gets the candy for the unruly child.

Many people think that because we work with adults, they are more mature and will express their desires in a more adult manner than throwing a fit. Our experience over the years has been that adults can actually be worse than children in many cases. See how the parent in the following example handled herself when she couldn't get her way:

Marge, a parent who had worked to organize an afterschool academic club, approached the principal of a neighborhood school to get permission to have dedicated space in that school for the tuition-based club to meet. The principal worked to find a suitable space for the program. After the first meeting of the academic club, Marge was not happy with the space. She asked the principal to move the program to a better room, a space currently occupied by an after school daycare program. Marge said that she had taken it upon herself to look at all of the facilities at the school, assessed that the program wasn't using the room as well as her academic program could, and found a better space for the after school daycare program. The principal explained to Marge that the afterschool daycare program was assigned that space and it would not be moved. Marge became very upset and told the principal that she was not happy with this decision.

Marge asked for a meeting with the district superintendent, Jennifer, about the situation. In this meeting Marge expressed her opinion about the principal and tried to influence Jennifer to overturn the principal's decision. Jennifer held firm even though Marge attacked the principal's motivation for the decision and insulted Jennifer for backing her principal. She left the office angry and upset.

Marge then started talking with members of the community and told them that Jennifer and the building principal favored the daycare program over her academic club. Marge was a member of several service clubs and at their meetings shared her disgust with everyone who would listen. She asked influential community members to call Jennifer and express their concerns with her decision. Finally, Marge showed up at a board meeting and put her name down to present during the public comment section of the meeting. She stood up in front of the community members present at the meeting and shared her disgust with the decision. Luckily, Jennifer had talked with her board chair and other members of the board and told them about the incident and her reasoning behind her decision. The board chair addressed the situation right after her presentation and told her that the board supported Jennifer's decision. She argued with the board chair and continued her complaints for several months behind Jennifer and the board's backs. Finally, when members of the community realized that she was the one in the wrong and stopped listening to her, she gave up on her quest to overturn the decision by Jennifer.

In analyzing this situation, you can see that Marge was not going to let go of her issue until she was satisfied or until she didn't get outside support. It wasn't until she tried to get the board to side with her and found out that she didn't have any support that she decided to give up her quest to get her way. Most people have a threshold of how far they will take an issue or complaint before giving up on it. Until they do give up, they may get more and more negative and obnoxious as they move up the levels to override your decision. Helping your board members understand this and keep it in mind when dealing with members of the public can help you avoid issues such as this when confronted by angry or negative people.

Key Point #2: At times, people who have strong beliefs or negative feelings may have trouble easily letting them go. Don't try to make people let go of strong feelings too quickly. Give them time and space to begin to soften their position on issues.

In general, keep the following in mind when working with difficult people:

- They may have become difficult because of some outside pressures or experiences; what you have done may not be the major factor causing them to give you a hard time.
- With some adults their negative behavior may mirror the "fit throwing" behaviors exhibited by some children.

- If they don't like your decision on an issue and they feel strongly about the issue, chances are good that they'll try to appeal to the next higher group. In most cases that means the board of education.
- Try not to take their negative behavior personally; if someone else were superintendent it's likely they'd be doing the same thing in a similar situation.

UNDERSTANDING THE PERSPECTIVES OF OTHERS

Put yourself in the "shoes" of the person receiving the message in order to "tailor" your communication to fit this person's needs. When our communication matches needs, people are better able to hear the message. Consider the following:

- Receiver's role
- Background and education
- Possible life experiences
- Communication style
- Person's needs and interests
- Person's understanding of the situation

Use the template in Figure 8.1 to help you as you plan to consider another person's perspective when dealing with an issue or situation.

Figure 8.1 Perspective Planning Template

Use the following template to plan how you will consider another person's perspective as you prepare to work more effectively with them.

Name: _____

Situation: _____

Describe the role of this person in relation to the situation (e.g., parent, community member, etc.)

_____

How does this role impact this person's perspective on the issue?

_____

_____

(Continued)

Figure 8.1 (Continued)

What is the person's background and education?

_____

_____

How might this background impact their perception on the situation?

_____

_____

Knowing what you know about this person, what kinds of life experiences do you think he or she may have had that helped to shape his or her perception of the position related to the situation?

_____

_____

_____

What do you need to do in relation to their possible perceptions in order to work effectively with them?

_____

_____

_____

What is this person's communication style?

_____

_____

_____

Does he or she tend to use a lot of words? Do you think he or she communicates better in verbal or written manner?

_____

_____

_____

How do you plan to use your understanding of his or her communication to make the best of the situation?

_____

_____

_____

What needs and interests does this person bring to the situation?

_____

_____

_____

How do you see these impacting your interactions with them?

_____

_____

_____

What level of understanding does this person bring to the situation?

_____

_____

_____

How do you see this level of understanding impacting your interactions? How can you effectively deal with this person in a positive and productive manner?

_____

_____

_____

Key Point #3: Take some time to think about the background experiences of the people you are working with. You may get some ideas related to how they attained their perceptions and ideas.

TYPES OF CONFLICT

Conflict is one of the behaviors that many people tend to avoid. A lot of people fear conflict. At times conflict can be good for groups and organizations if it productive and is directed at real issues. In schools, we experience two types of conflict.

Substantive (Cognitive) Conflict

At times groups engage in conflict based on principle, information, and actual content. Researchers have called this type of conflict substantive or cognitive conflict. In working to resolve this type of conflict, leaders need to provide guidance and structures to help people focus on the major issues and find ways to work through differences. Effective leaders might divide people into groups, ask them to provide their rationale in written form, break a decision into various parts, and so on. In the end the job is to help keep groups focused on the substance of the issue and support people as they work through these issues. Substantive conflict utilizes the following:

- **Stable conflict energy:** When engaged in substantive conflict, parties usually experience balanced and consistent conflict energy.
- **Stable relationships and atmosphere:** Since the conflict is focused on the substance of content of the decision, relationships are maintained. The atmosphere in which the conflict occurs also is stable.
- **Lots of information by the group to examine issues and make decisions:** Substantive conflict uses three times the amount of information used by groups in affective conflict to make decisions.
- **Conflict resolution through focus:** Conflicts are resolved by staying focused on the issue and working through the problem. (Based on Guetzkow & Gyr, 1954, in Folger, Poole, & Stutman, 1993)

Leaders can spot substantive conflict in the groups they work with because the issues are focused on topics rather than personalities. It is important to try to keep a group focused in the content of a decision because as the conflict continues over time, it could become easy for a group to slip into affect (personality-based) conflict.

Affective (Personality-Based) Conflict

Groups working through conflict may also focus more on personalities and relationships during their disagreement. This type of conflict is referred to as affective or personality-based conflict. In affective conflict a group is not focused on solving the issue but interested in "attacking" others. Some of the characteristics and attributes of a group in affective conflict include the following:

- **Extreme frustration:** Since group members start to get angry at others based on their personality characteristics, extreme frustration can set in.
- **Likely to exhibit spiraling escalation:** Since there are limited solutions to the issues expressed in the conflict they tend to get worse and more personal as time evolves. Spiraling escalation refers to the fact that the conflict normally doesn't get resolved and keeps going back to the beginning without ever being resolved.
- **Highly correlated with poor relationships and emotional atmosphere:** Because conflicts are personal in nature, relationships tend to be compromised.
- **Groups tend to engage in "flight or fight" to reach consensus:** It is hard for these groups to reach consensus since there are disagreeing on personality-based subjects. (Based on Guetzkow & Gyr, 1954, in Folger, Poole, & Stutman, 1993)

Key Point #4: Understanding the specific type of conflict can help you decide how to support those people in your district.

SKILLS FOR DEALING WITH DIFFICULT PEOPLE

Temporary Suspension of Opinion

Temporary suspension of opinion is a skill that you can selectively use when you want to allow another person to express themselves or work through a problem. It involves listening and truly trying to understand the other person before you make any comments. We first encountered the skill as it was outlined by Edgar Schein (1997). He suggests that we suspend our own impulses to respond and give the other person time to share his or her thoughts. In using this skill in real life situations we have found the following:

- People are able to get their frustrations "off their chest" and empty emotions that are holding them back from listening.
- Individuals are able to "hear" the description of what is bothering them and many times can begin to solve their own issues and problems.

- Angry people see that you respect them enough to truly listen to their concerns with an open mind. This helps them to de-escalate their emotions and begin to connect with you.
- The person suspending judgment is usually able to better understand the perspective of the person talking and then able to develop a strategy to help him or her to resolve their problem or issue.
- Interactions become more intentional and less reactionary in nature; both parties benefit from the increased cooperative atmosphere.

The use of temporary suspension of opinion helps all parties in the relationship to feel respected and understood. Here are two powerful examples of how it looks in action:

Mike, a superintendent in a medium-sized school district, encounters an angry and upset community member regarding the decision to close school early in response to the threat of bad weather. As the parent started to share his anger, Mike's natural inclination was to defend his decision. Instead, Mike just listened. As the conversation progressed the parent shared that he was upset because he didn't receive notification of the early dismissal and his children went home to an empty house. Now Mike understood the concern. He worked with the parent to talk about notification procedures. The parent left the meeting feeling much better about the situation.

If Mike had responded right away to the parent and tried to defend his decision (as he had done so many times in the past) he would have missed the core of the concern. By temporarily suspending his impulse to respond he was able to find out the exact nature of the concern, then talk with the parent about strategies to deal with the situation. By temporarily suspending his opinion, Mike de-escalated the emotions of the parent and was able to get to the bottom of the situation.

Samantha, a superintendent in a school district, was at a monthly board meeting when the following situation arose:

As Samantha was getting ready to ask for a board vote on an issue, one of the members shared a concern he had about the proposal. The opportunity for discussion had just ended and Samantha could have told the board member it was too late to bring up a concern. She had worked with her board chair and the other members of the board in advance to identify their issues and concerns, but this request came out of the blue. She decided to suspend her opinion and asked the board chair if the issue could be addressed. She then asked the board member to tell her more details about the concern. He brought up two or three issues, which she addressed to his satisfaction. The proposal passed unanimously.

The second example is more complex that the first one. Samantha had worked with her board on the proper protocol for addressing questions and concerns, but this situation just came up. She chose to suspend her opinion (and not lecture the board member) in order to address the situation. Her action allowed the member to save face in the public and she was able to get unanimous agreement on the proposal. If she had gone through with her initial impulse to publicly remind him of the protocol, she risked alienating him for the future.

Once the board meeting was over, she scheduled time with the board member to make sure the two of them reviewed the proper protocol for addressing concerns at board meetings. Over the next few months she took a little extra time with this board member to ensure his concerns were addressed before meetings.

Temporary suspension of opinion can be a difficult skill to learn and practice. Most of us got into education because of our interest in being helpful to others, so holding our opinion can be difficult. In our staff development sessions with leaders on this topic, we have seen people utilize some of the following strategies to help them as they attempt to use temporary suspension of opinion:

- Listening carefully to what the other person is saying as if you might be required to repeat it in the future.
- Looking directly at the person who is talking, concentrating on their facial expressions and nonverbal gestures.
- Holding your hands behind your back and concentrating on the speaker (this is good for leaders who talk with their hands).
- Working to mentally draw an outline of the major topics in your head as the speaker is talking.
- "Biting your lip" (literally) as you are listening to the speaker.
- Trying to sum up what the speaker is saying.

Even though suspension of opinion can be a difficult skill to learn and master, it will help you to set and maintain a respectful situation as you work with difficult people.

Key Point #5: Temporarily withholding your opinion can allow people the time needed to think about and work through their issues. It also gives you time to think about your own response to a situation.

Framing

Another skill that can help you manage difficult people is the skill of framing. Framing involves using language in order to draw the boundaries around a discussion or conflict. Framing can help you establish yourself as the person in charge of the conversation and keep groups and individuals inside of set parameters.

In the following example, listen to how Bob used framing to set the boundaries in a discussion with a parent group regarding a situation with a staff member:

> Thank you for coming tonight. I'm sure most of you have heard about the legal situation with Mrs. Smith. I called this meeting to share with you the factual information regarding Mrs. Smith's situation so that you can understand how it impacts your children. There are also several rumors floating around the community. I can only share the factual information that I am allowed to divulge related to the employee information statute used in our state; I will not go beyond that level nor will I take any questions related to rumors or information I am legally bound not to share..."

In this example, Bob sets the frame for the meeting and draws a parameter around the discussion. He is very clear and does not leave the impression that he is negotiable about this situation. If someone wants him to go beyond the boundaries he can just remind the group of his initial frame. This protects him but also keeps the emotions in check.

In many cases your framing statement won't be associated with situations as serious as the one faced by Bob. Here's another framing example with a less serious situation:

> Norma was talking to a group of paraprofessionals about the new school year calendar. She started the meeting by stating: "I know many of you may have questions about certain aspects of this calendar. Before talking about those aspects, I want to present the entire calendar to you first. This will allow you to see the big picture and allow me to explain the rationale for certain decisions. Once I am finished with my presentation, I will ask you to meet in small groups and generate a list of the positive aspects of the calendar and a list of your concerns. Once this has been completed, we will compile both lists and I will share responses to your concerns."

Norma put the framing statement together because of her previous experiences with this normally reactive group. In the past her meetings with them had erupted into situations where it was "her against the entire group." Some members of the group enjoyed the fact that Norma had been put on the spot. Her frame was intended to set up a situation where positive resolution of concerns could be done in the meeting.

So far we have seen how framing can be used in group situations. It can be a very valuable tool for working with difficult or angry individuals. Let's see how Roberta uses framing as she approaches a conference with an angry parent:

> Roberta had received a phone call from an angry parent whose child had been left off at the wrong stop by the bus driver. The parent wanted to come in to talk about the issue. Roberta started out the conference by saying, "I want to find out all of your concerns so as you talk I plan to listen and write down the pertinent details. Once you are completely finished I'll use what I've gathered to talk with you about how we will resolve the situation. Even though you may still be upset, I'll expect you to listen as I share my perspective on the situation. Once we are in agreement, we will work together to generate a plan to keep this from happening in the future."

The frame here helped Roberta set parameters so the conversation could be civil, plus quickly get to solutions for the problem. It may appear that in her opening statement Roberta is harsh with the parent but she is firm in setting boundaries for the conversation. These boundaries help to ensure the conversation will move toward resolution of the problem. Roberta will listen intently to what the parent is telling her even if she wants to respond. Once the parent finishes, Roberta then shares her perspective. If the parent does not respect Roberta's time to respond and interrupts her, Roberta will remind her of the parameters of the conversation. If the parent refuses to follow the parameters, Roberta can remind her, but if the conversation gets out of hand, she can also call an end to the conversation. Roberta has set parameters to ensure reasonableness in the conversation; she can end the conversation if it becomes unreasonable. Roberta is in control and sets the tone for the resolution of the problem.

Here are some examples of starter framing statements for you to consider as you face situations requiring you to set the boundaries with others:

- "Today, we are here to talk about . . ."
- "The major points we need to address are . . ."
- "Even though there are other new topics that we could consider, we need to . . ."
- "Since we have limited time in this meeting . . ."
- "I know you may be wondering about . . . but today we are here to . . . "
- "As you talk I plan to just listen so I understand . . ."
- "You want to keep talking about the past but we need to focus on the future."
- "As I see it, there are three issues we need to focus on . . ."
- "I know in the past you have . . . but now we will focus on . . ."

Reflecting Skills

Sometimes your work with difficult people will be enhanced through the use of reflecting. Reflecting involves letting the person who sent you the message (through talking) know that you have received and understand it. This skill is similar to paraphrasing but it involves a more direct response than paraphrasing does. We've found it to be helpful in working with difficult or angry people because of its directness; it seems to match their emotion better than a nice, indirect statement. You have to use what you are most comfortable with when you work with angry or difficult people. Table 8.1 outlines the difference between reflecting and paraphrasing statements.

There are several reflecting statement types we use in our work with others. Three types that we focus on are listed below:

Content: Returning what the sender told you in a slightly different form than it was said to you.

- "You shared the three main . . ."
- "Your major concerns seem to be . . ."
- "You said . . ."

Emotion: Reflecting back the emotion you perceive the sender is feeling.

- "This is very upsetting to you . . ."
- "You are feeling stress . . ."
- "You are frustrated by . . ."

Chunking: Reflecting back a stream of content you've received and combined together to assist the sender in seeing the whole picture.

- "The three major points she made were . . ."

Table 8.1   Example of Paraphrasing and Reflecting Statements

Paraphrasing Statements	Reflecting Statements
"I feel you are saying that you don't understand."	"You don't understand."
"It seems to me that you are confused."	"You are confused."
"I hear you saying that you have three issues with my comments."	"You have three issues with my comments."
"You appear to me to be angry."	"You are angry."
"I hear you saying you want ..."	"You want ..."

- "The first idea you shared was . . . The second . . ."
- "In general you have . . ."

Key Point #6: Effective framing statements help to constrain conversations and put you in control. Reflecting statements help the other party to hear that you understand their perspective. Both of these elements help to set and maintain a collaborative relationship.

Implementation Blocking

In new projects or implementations, it is normal for some people to be uncomfortable. At times, some people may actually lose something as a result of the implementation. These people may try to stop or slow the progress of the project. One strategy that is employed is called implementation blocking. Here is a brief definition we have developed for this behavior:

A process where member(s) of a group try to slow or block a change through the use of comments that undermine the confidence of the leader.

There are several steps that you can do in order to deal with implementation blocking:

- Recognize implementation blocking is happening
- Listen to the message, ask clarification questions, seek to understand the nature and origin of the concern
- Listen for the core of the concern
- Listen for specific language, be careful about vague or general statements

Shifting Energy Focus

Incidents where there are public displays of difficult or negative behavior can take you by surprise and can be hard to deal with in a positive manner. There are ways to effectively shift the energy focus away from you so you can think and figure out how to diminish the level of anxiety and conflict present. We'll introduce some of the more common ones we have used and taught others in our development of leadership principles over the years.

- Use of gestures: Gestures effectively work well to help move negative energy away from you when you are in a conflict. Gestures communicate directly with the subconscious of those we are

Table 8.2   Practice With Implementation Blocking

Try the steps out with the following implementation blocking statements:		
Statement	**Manipulation Attempt**	**Strategies/ Statements**
"Many of us on the staff are wondering why this initiative went forward without more discussion."		
"I've been talking to other staff and parents who share my concerns . . ."		
"The informal leaders of the building met and have talked about what is wrong with this project."		

SOURCE: Adapted from Eller, *Effective Group Facilitation in Education,* 2004.

working with and provide a powerful way to shift negative energy away when it's necessary. Here are some common gestures and their impact:

- o   Hand held out, palm facing audience: Stop.
- o   Pointing to group: You.
- o   Point to self: Me.
- o   Hand passing by group in semi-circular motion: We're all in this together.

- Placing controversial information on charts or screens: If you have controversial information to share (like budget cut lists, sport reductions, and so on), place that information on charts or project them on a screen. As you get ready to share this information, stand off to the side and review the list or even allow people to read it over silently. Since the major focus will be the list, that's where the initial negative energy will be directed. After the initial energy is spent or used to react to the posted information, come back into the picture and move forward.

- Stand in or sit in the audience during emotional times: If you are closer to people they don't have to raise their voices in order to be heard when they have questions or concerns. People tend to feel you are more human when they can see your eyes and are close to you.

DESIGN AND IMPLEMENT POSITIVE PROBLEM-SOLVING PROCESSES

One basis for you to be successful in working with difficult people is to develop and operate from a problem-solving process. In the districts where we have worked this is one of the first things that we did. Normally these kinds of processes cover problems in all parts of the organization.

For example, we normally develop and implement a multistep process for working through conflict. This process is fairly straightforward but provides a good foundation for you to build upon in your own district.

Figure 8.2 Sample Problem-Solving Process

In the Achievement Valley School District, we believe in partnerships with our parents and community in order to best educate our students. In that endeavor, conflicts and disagreements may come up from time to time. In order to build the kind of partnerships that best serve our students and to model appropriate behavior for our children we believe in a problem-resolution process.

In this problem-resolution process, issues will be handled at the earliest possible time and at the level of the organization closest to the origin of the problem. As a school district we will follow these steps in resolving conflicts and problems:

1. We understand that conflict is a natural part of the interactive process when people work together. We will work to identify the cause of the problem and develop plans to remedy it and move our relationship back to the positive side as soon as possible.

2. If a problem arises within a classroom setting, the complainant will be directed back to that level to work out the situation with the classroom teacher.

3. If the issue cannot be resolved at the classroom level, the complainant will be directed back to the principal to address the situation from the school building level.

4. If the issue still cannot be resolved, the complainant will be directed to work out the issue at the district level. The resolution will be accommodated by the superintendent or his or her designee.

5. If the issue still cannot be resolved, the complainant will be directed to work with the Board of Education chair. The board chair will work with all parties to ensure the situation is resolved in a positive manner.

MEDIATING CONFLICT

You may encounter situations where the level of conflict between two people escalates to that the point that it significantly keeps them from being able to work together effectively. In some cases these people need to find a way to work out their differences. In other cases you may be able to help them to find a way to get along. Be careful when thinking about getting involved in other people's conflicts though. You can be drawn into a situation that you may not be able to manage. Here are some considerations you should think about before getting involved in mediating a conflict between two parties:

- Make sure both parties are interested in having their conflict mediated.
- Make sure they trust you to be their mediator.
- Assess your skill and interest in serving as a mediator; if you are not feeling very strong in the role, you will not be able to serve the parties in conflict well.

If you choose to mediate conflict it is important to have steps or a process in place that helps guide you through the process. Consider the template in Figure 8.3 as a possible guide.

> **Key Point #7:** When choosing to mediate, be sure to carefully assess the situation to see if you will be able to effectively deal with the situation and still come out as an interested third party. At times people who have tried to mediate have lost in the exchange because rather than fix the situation they just made both parties angry.

Figure 8.4 (p. 170) provides a clear way to work with people in conflict in a productive manner. A written plan helps to keep everyone on track and positive.

WORKING POSITIVELY WITH THE PRESS

In some communities, the local newspaper can be an extremely positive force or your worst enemy. Many superintendents work hard to build a positive relationship with the press. Here are some of the strategies we have seen over the years:

- Establish regular meetings with newspaper staff.
- Build a professional relationship with the local newspaper editor.

Figure 8.3 Mediation Process

When you choose to help the parties involved in the conflict work through their issues, consider the following steps.

- Be sure that all parties in conflict are in the room.
- Place yourself somewhat between the conflicting parties, but avoid sitting in the direct line of emotional fire.
- Open the conversation by stating your awareness of the problem or situation, and state why you are getting involved and have asked them to come together.
- Set the ground rules for the interaction and communication in the meeting (no name calling, listening while the other person is talking, and so on).
- Open the session by asking one of the parties in conflict to state his, her or their perspective while the other party listens; be sure to take notes of what was presented.
- Allow the other person or party to share his, her, or their side of the story in regard to the conflict.
- During the time the parties are describing the situation, make no comments that would appear that you have taken a side or formed an opinion.
- Summarize what you have heard so far, and ask the parties in conflict to share their perception of what has caused the conflict.
- Ask the parties to state what they would like to see happen in order for the conflict to be resolved.
- Summarize what you have heard up to this point; ask participants to agree on a plan to resolve this conflict.
- Help the parties in conflict develop a follow up plan to make sure it stays on track; discuss possible situations where the plan could run into trouble.

During your session, be careful not to get pulled into the conflict, take sides, or solve the problem for the participants. Be sure to find ways to protect yourself from the negative energy that the individuals in conflict will be emitting during this discussion.

SOURCE: From Eller, *Effective Group Facilitation in Education*, 2004, p. 87

- Offer to write a regular column in the paper highlighting district operations and events.
- Write up events for the local paper to publish.
- Invite members of the press to school events.
- Host quarterly open meetings with members of the school district staff and the press.
- Invite members of the press to district staff development opportunities.
- Identify a community relations person as a point person for information.
- Assign principals periodic columns and public TV appearances.

Figure 8.4 Personal Conflict Resolution Template

At times, we all find ourselves in situations where we have a personal conflict with another person. You may decide it's in the best interest of you and your district to attempt to work through the issue with the other person. When you are trying to work through a conflict with another person, consider the following steps:

- **Body positioning:** Place yourself in a position where your body position will set the tone you wish to set. For example, if you want to set a collaborative tone, sit next to the other person; if you want to let them know even though you are interested in working things out you are still the boss, sit across from them, etc.

- **Frame the purpose of the discussion:** Start off with a framing statement to set the parameters and the tone of the session.

- **Ground rules:** Set the ground rules that you and the other person in the meeting will follow (no name calling, listening while the other person is talking, and so on).

- **Starting the session:** Open the session by asking the person or people you are meeting with to share the core of their concerns; what he, she, or they are looking for as a result of this meeting; share your thoughts as well.

- **Track the conversation and main points:** As the other person is talking, take notes to help you track the major points being made.

- **Temporarily suspend your opinion:** During the time the other person is describing the situation, make no comments that would communicate that you are not listening.

- **Sum it up:** Summarize what you heard and the major points that were made by the other party.

- **Your perspective:** Share your perspective on the issue, hitting the main points in a factual manner.

- **Get to the point:** Examine the core of what you and the other party have shared; look for common points of agreement; summarize the main points of discussion.

- **Develop a plan:** Either share a plan or work to develop a plan to resolve the issue; make sure the plan incorporates effort from both parties and is specific with follow up strategies and ways to measure its success.

SUMMARY

Working with negative people and groups can be both rewarding and challenging to you as the superintendent. Even though the behaviors these people exhibit may seem to be random in nature they usually follow some predictable pattern. Once you can begin to see these problems as natural and part of working with others, your view of difficult or negative people can change.

As you think about the content of this chapter, reflect on the following questions:

- What makes people negative or difficult to work with? How does knowing some of these causes help us in our work with them?
- Why is it difficult to try to change the minds of negative or difficult people? What strategies can be employed to help with these kinds of situations?
- How can you deal with negative elements of the press?
- How can you protect yourself and move toward a productive relationship as you relate to negative people?

There will always be negative people around to provide you with challenges and opportunities. We hope the strategies and ideas presented in this book will prepare you for success as you take on this never-ending phenomenon in your district.

In Chapter 9, Getting the Word Out: Effective Communication Strategies, you will learn how to effectively manage communication that originates from your office to the various constituents in your district. This information will assist you as you tackle the difficult task of making sure communication is accurate and effective.

9

Getting the Word Out

Effective Communication Strategies

> *It is not so much the content of what one says as the way*
> *in which one says it. However important the thing you say,*
> *what's the good of it if not heard or, being heard, not felt.*
> —Sylvia Ashton-Warner

Effective communication is essential for your survival as a new superintendent. Unfortunately most of your constituents likely have had minimal personal communication experience in the past with school superintendents. Many of those that do have short interactions with you or talk to you under somewhat stressed situations when people are angry or want to influence you about a policy or decision. As a new superintendent you need to make the most of every communication opportunity.

ABOUT THIS CHAPTER

The content in this chapter is designed to help you maximize communication opportunities. Below are effective communication and information management topics we will cover:

- Strategies to make your communication more effective

- Ideas to help you as you track and manage the flow of information to and from your office and in the district
- Strategies to improve superintendent–board communication
- Ideas for dealing with confidential private information and information of a more public nature

THE POWER OF EFFECTIVE COMMUNICATION

Since the bulk of the communication opportunities you will have are short and unpredictable, you'll need to make the most of every interaction. In order to prepare, it is important for you to think about how you want to portray yourself as the leader of the school district. Your communications

Figure 9.1   Focusing Your Values and Beliefs

1. What are your cores values and beliefs?

2. Why did you choose to become a superintendent?

3. What parts of your values and beliefs do you have trouble justifying or defending when situations become difficult?

    How do you find the inner strength to continue to defend them in these circumstances?

4. What values and beliefs have become stronger over the years as a result of your experiences in education?

need to be purposeful and focused. Below is a process some successful superintendents use to help focus their communications.

1. **Identify your core values.**

In order to be able to communicate in an effective manner, it is crucial for you to know what you stand for as a school leader. If you clearly understand your values and beliefs you will be better able to design and deliver clear and focused communications. This knowledge will not only help you plan effective communications but will also help you react when you are surprised by the press, community members, parents, and others you communicate with.

Key Point #1: Identifying your core values is essential to effective communication. It allows you to think and focus.

2. **Focus your essential messages.**

Since you will be communicating with most of your constituents in short, periodic messages it is important for you to plan and rehearse messages that convey your core values. People in sales call these the "thirty second" messages. They rehearse short messages that can be communicated in thirty seconds or less and delivered when needed. You might think that planning your messages sounds manipulative but unlike sales, you are not rehearsing your messages to change behavior; you are rehearsing them to make your message clearer. Table 9.1 shows some examples of focused essential messages that we have heard superintendents use over the years in specific situations.

Table 9.1   Samples of Short, Focused Messages Used by Superintendents

General Topic	Sample of Focused Message
Student Achievement	"All students can learn if given the proper environment and support."
Food Service	"We offer a highly nutritious, cost-effective meal that is appealing to students."
Budget	"In our district, funds are focused on classrooms and students."
Decision Making	"All decisions made in this district are made in the best interest of students."
Maintenance	"We will maintain our buildings and protect the investment our community has in its schools."

Some of these statements may sound like mission or vision statements but these were designed using the core values and beliefs of each superintendent. When encountering situations where time is short, having thought through your essential communications can help you stay focused and on track. If you have more time, you can expand your essential messages and add in more details.

Identifying these essential messages allows you to develop a foundation or base upon which to build a more complex message. When you encounter difficulties regarding programming, budgeting, or one of the other distractions common in the superintendency, you can go back to your essential messages to reground yourself and move forward on a variety of issues.

Many new superintendents think they know what their essential messages are and that they can access them instantly if they need to in a communication situation. We have found that this is a skill they often need to practice and refine throughout their tenure. Figure 9.2 illustrates a process that will help you identify and focus your essential messages as a new superintendent.

> **Key Point #2:** Focusing your key messages allows you to be prepared when you are asked to clarify or justify your position on issues in either public or private settings.

3. Plan your responses to typical situations you may face.
Superintendents are very principle-centered people. They usually have clear focus and don't get taken off track too easily unless they are surprised by people or events. We have seen colleagues who are normally very centered make communication errors as a result of being taken by surprise. Effective superintendents think through possible outcomes of policies or decisions, and then design essential message responses to unforeseen situations. These superintendents usually involve their leadership team in helping them identify the potential problems and their essential message responses to these problems. Involving the administrative team in this type of exercise not only helps you to think of all of the possible problems associated with a situation, but helps get other members of the team engaged in developing solutions and on board with the same message. This is essential for your survival as a new superintendent. Getting everyone together to talk about essential messages and typical problem situations can be as simple as asking people to meet or as complex as going on a mini-retreat to generate ideas. Some of our colleagues in the past have found it helpful to use some type of instrument or

Figure 9.2 Focusing Your Essential Messages

What are the areas of school operation where you think you will need focused, clear messages? (transportation program, student learning, etc.)

Within each of these areas, list the key words or phrases that you want to include in your essential messages.

Area 1

Area 2

Area 3

Area 4

Within each of your most important areas, write an essential message that you could deliver in 30 seconds.

Area 1

Area 2

Area 3

Area 4

Review each of your essential messages; refine them as needed.

Area 1

Area 2

Area 3

Area 4

process for identifying and brainstorming ideas. Sticky Note Ripple Effects is one method you may find helpful.

Sticky Note Ripple Effects

This activity, introduced in the book *Energizing Staff Meetings* (Eller & Eller, 2006), has helped groups generate many ideas and possible scenarios based on a decision or policy. A variation of it is offered here to help you identify possible community responses to decisions or policies so that you can plan how to tailor your essential messages to fit the specific situations.

Here's how the activity works:

- A chart is placed on the wall that contains a large drawing of a pond with ripples similar to Figure 9.3.
- In the center of the "pond" the decision or policy to be implemented is written.
- Members of the administrative team are given "sticky notes" and asked to write down as many stakeholder reactions to the proposed decision or policy as they can think of.
- After a short period of time (five to ten minutes), members of the administrative team are asked to post their sticky notes on the chart. Those reactions that are stronger or could have a potentially more immediate negative impact on the policy or decision are placed near the center of the chart. Reactions that are less likely to have an immediate negative affect on the policy or decision are placed in the outer "ripples" of the chart.

Figure 9.3 Example of a Blank Sticky Note Ripple Effects Chart

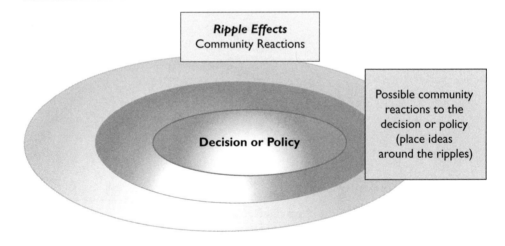

- Once all the sticky notes are posted on the chart, the person leading the meeting reads through them and the group decides if their placement on the charts is appropriate.

- When the group has reached agreement that the reactions are accurately placed, they generate possible essential message responses that can be delivered publicly.

- The essential messages are written down so that the superintendent or key members of the administrative team can remember them when needed.

As you can see from Figure 9.4 there are some community reactions that are more serious or potentially damaging in nature than others. As mentioned earlier, a team using this process would next take the top four or five reactions and generate essential messages based on the most crucial needs of the public. Figure 9.5 shows examples of essential messages based on possible public reactions from Figure 9.4.

4. Think through how you will deal with major objections to your essential messages.

In any school district, there are constituents on all sides of a particular issue. If you try to improve your bus service, you may be diminishing another program in the school district to get the funding to improve the bus routes, so you may have a group of people against your plan

Figure 9.4 Sample of a Completed Sticky Note Ripple Effects Chart

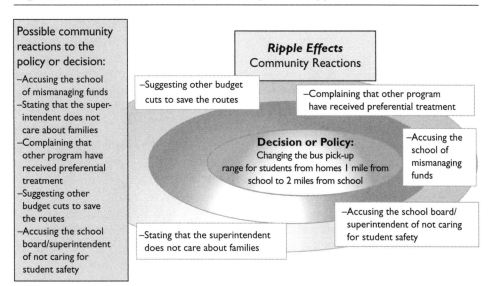

SOURCE: From Eller & Eller, *Energizing Staff Meetings*, (2006).

Table 9.2   Sample Essential Messages

Possible Public Reaction to the Decision or Policy	Possible Essential Messages
Accusing the school board/ superintendent of not caring for student safety	We care about the safety of our students. We have looked at every stop and assessed that there are no negative impacts based on our decision.
Accusing the school of mismanaging funds	We constantly evaluate each program to make sure that every program has a high cost/benefit ratio. Those that are not giving us much bang for our buck are scaled back or reduced.
Stating that the superintendent does not care about families	Students are at the top of our decision-making processes in this district. We care about families and try to balance a variety of factors when making a decision or program adjustment.

to improve bus service. As a new superintendent you must have strategies in place to deal with major objections to your communications. One strategy is to identify possible objections.

To use this strategy, identify possible objections and provide rationale for why those objections don't make sense. Some of you may know of this strategy by a name used in the sales industry: kill the objections. In general it involves the speaker (or salesperson, which may seem like one of your roles as superintendent) actually naming the possible objections then providing rationale for why the objections do not hold merit or would not be good choices for the decision. See how Ben, the superintendent in the following example, uses this principle to deal with a message he has to deliver to a group:

> We have had to move forward on our decision to change boundary lines to equalize the population in our elementary schools. I know many of you might be thinking, "Why didn't we select another option?" Let me share some of the other possible options and why we didn't choose them. First, we looked at building a new school. (Shares the reasons why this option was not good). Next, we looked at canceling open enrollment commitments. (Shares reasons why this option did not address the situation). We examined moving sixth-grade students to the middle schools. (Shares reasons why this option did not address the situation). (Shares other possible options and why they were taken out of consideration).

Figure 9.5 Communication of Objections Planning Template

List the major points to be addressed in your announcement or communication.

_____

_____

_____

_____

In relation to your major points, what kinds of objections or counterpoints might members of the public or representatives of special interest groups hold and be willing to share in a public meeting to discredit your major points?

_____

_____

_____

_____

Develop an outline of your announcement incorporating your major points and containing information to "kill" their objections or oppositional points. Be clear and specific.

_____

_____

_____

_____

What information or data will you need in order to make your point and deal with their objections? Where will you get this information or data?

_____

_____

_____

_____

As you can see in this example, Ben was able to talk with the group about their possible concerns and deal with these objections. In utilizing this strategy, it is important to try to anticipate the group's objections before they are brought forward. This keeps you out of a defensive mode and in control of the communication. Let's look at how another superintendent, Bill, gets put on the defensive as he delivers the same message Ben did in the first example, but neglects to address the objections before the group brings them up:

> We have decided to move forward with changing boundary lines for our elementary schools in order equalize the imbalance of our school populations. We think this will be the best choice for our schools in the long run. Someone from the audience raises his hand. Bill calls on the person, who asks, "What about building a new school in the region, did you look at that option?" Bill responds, "Yes, we did look at that possibility but it didn't seem to be the right option to solve our problem at this point." Audience members raise their hands and ask further questions about why building a new school would not help the situation. Bill answers the questions but becomes nervous and feels slightly defensive. Another committee member raises her hand and asks, "What about moving the sixth-grade students to the middle school, wouldn't that help our situation?" Bill responds, "Moving students to the middle school could lower our elementary enrollments but then our middle schools could be overcrowded." Community member asks Bill a question about the potential class sizes if sixth-grade students were moved to the middle school. Bill responds, "I'm not sure of the exact numbers if we were to choose that scenario." By now Bill is feeling like he is being attacked by the group and has to defend his choices.

Obviously, we'd all like to deal with situations more like Ben and avoid confrontations such as Bill experienced in his example. By thinking through, being prepared for, and "killing objections" before they happen, you go along way toward making your communications less subject to attacks. You also help keep yourself out of defensive positions when you make announcements to others. In order to stay out of trouble, it is important to think through your messages and the possible objections they could face. Figure 9.5 contains a planning template you will find helpful as you begin to think through how to anticipate and deal with objections to your messages.

An example of a completed form that Sharon, a new superintendent, recently used to plan for a meeting where she was going to make an announcement that would prompt several objections is shown in Figure 9.6.

Key Point #3: Being ready to deal with objections allows you to seamlessly answer concerns without looking defensive.

Figure 9.6 Completed Communication of Objections Planning Template

List the major points to be addressed in your announcement or communication.

I'm planning to make an announcement that the district will pursue offering all-day kindergarten during the next academic year. In order to offer this program we will need to reduce funding somewhere else in the school district. We are planning to reduce the breadth of our high school offerings in order to come up with the money that will be needed to hire six additional teachers to implement the all-day kindergarten initiative. In delivering this plan, I will need to address the following points:

Why it is important to offer all-day kindergarten

How we will accommodate the extra classrooms in our elementary schools

What reductions will be made at the high school to generate the needed funding

What we hope to accomplish as a result of this change

In relation to your major points, what kinds of objections or counterpoints might members of the public or representatives of special interest groups hold and be willing to share in a public meeting to discredit you?

This issue is very controversial but is needed by our school district. The following objections to this announcement may come up at our meeting:

Why do we need to go with an all-day kindergarten program?

Why should the high school program suffer because of this decision?

How will the decision be made regarding which programs will be reduced at the high school?

What other ways to generate funding have been discussed to support this new program?

Why can't kindergarten parents pay for the additional half-day?

Why can't kindergarten parents just enroll their children in day care programs?

How come other programs in the district have not been looked at for reductions in order to fund the all-day kindergarten initiative?

Develop an outline of your announcement incorporating your major points and containing information to "kill" their objections or oppositional points. Be clear and specific.

Meeting Outline

Provide an overview of the decision to offer all-day kindergarten.

Provide a framing statement that informs people that I want to go through all of the information regarding the decision first then open the floor for questions.

Provide a rationale regarding student achievement for the program.

(Continued)

Figure 9.6 (Continued)

Show a summary of parental interest in the program.

Outline of funding needs of the program.

Discuss where the funding for the program will be coming from.

Share the process that was used to identify all the possible areas where funding could be obtained to operate the program.

Discuss the major objections that are listed in step two of this planning template and how they were considered in making this decision.

Talk about why the decision to reduce some high school programming was made.

Share what programs may be reduced.

Discuss how courses with low or inadequate enrollment will be identified and reduced.

Present how much money will be generated through this process (use visuals to show the numbers).

Remind the group of the need, the process used for considering all options, and how the ultimate decision was made.

Open up the discussion for questions and comments.

What information or data will you need in order to make your point and deal with their objections? Where will you get this information or data?

In order to help me with the exact data that I need to present to the group, I will obtain student achievement information related to the entry-level skills of our five-year-old students, and how many of the students are still academically behind expectations at the end of second grade. I will also need to obtain research data about the benefits of all-day kindergarten. I can get these from my staff development director.

I will also need enrollment information from the last three years for the courses at the high school level that we are considering eliminating and the amount of money that we will save by not offering these courses. I also need to look at the teachers involved in these courses and what they will be teaching as a result of these changes. The high school principal can provide me with that information.

MANAGING INFORMATION FLOW IN YOUR OFFICE AND IN THE DISTRICT

As a new superintendent it's important for you manage the information flow to and from your office. You will be judged immediately on how accurate the information provided by your office is and its smooth flow. It's not enough for you to wish that this will happen or just tell people this is what you want. It is crucial for you to implement strategies immediately that will ensure you are on top of the information flow in your office. Below are some ideas you should consider in managing information flow:

Develop information flow charts: Since information flow is so crucial to your success, be sure to develop flow charts of who receives what information and when. These flow charts will help your staff get information out in a timely manner and make sure that no one needing the information is left off the list. It may take several charts to hit the major informational items that will impact your school district. You may need charts for information such as school closures, emergency or crisis information, school board information, "good news" information, student achievements, and other kinds of information that need to be channeled to your school community. With each of these situations, you may need an entirely different flow chart. An example of a flowchart is shown in Figure 9.7 so that you can see how this might be helpful in your district.

This basic structure can be duplicated to fit your needs and make sure everyone who needs to get information does so in a timely manner.

Regular meetings to talk about information flow with staff and your administrative team: Effective superintendents conduct regular meetings

Figure 9.7 School Closure Informational Flowchart

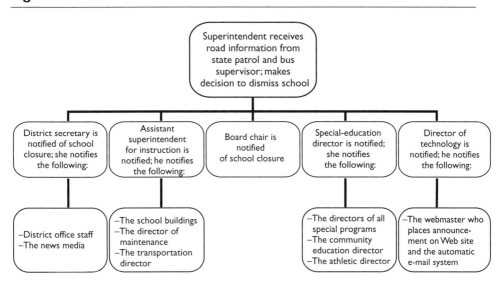

to discuss information flow. In these meetings they talk with their staff about how things are going related to information flow, new informational needs of constituents, new constituents and their need for information, and other issues that help with information flow.

Naming official information sources: In many school districts rumors have a tendency to get started quite easily. Someone hears a piece of information and whether or not it is true passes it on to others. Before you know it a rumor has started and could spin out of control. Superintendents can battle rumors by naming "official information sources" in their school districts. Examples of official sources we have seen used include the following:

- Designating that all announcements come from the school district information office
- Designating a school district newsletter as the official information source of the district
- Developing specific letterhead for committees and departments; designating that the only accurate news coming from these committees and departments will appear on their particular letterhead

Key Point #4: Information flow charts can be very helpful when you are facing situations that involve emotional information. They allow you to move forward in notifying key constituents and members of your community even in difficult times.

Establishing timetables for information releases: At the beginning of each school year some superintendents use the school calendar as a vehicle for releasing information on major school initiatives. By setting this up in advance district constituents know when certain announcements will occur and that if they hear information leaking out before these official notification dates, they are probably rumors. Table 9.3 shows an example of one school district's notification dates.

ESTABLISHING A BOARD COMMUNICATION PROCESS

There are several types of board communication. Some types are discussed in other parts of this book, but we will also highlight them in this chapter.

Table 9.3   Example of School District Notification Dates

Month	Typical Informational Announcements Made During the Month
July	School registration dates, student classroom supply lists, school open house dates, school board meeting dates, school board goals, staff development plan for upcoming year
August	New employees, student grade and class placements, school district calendar, school improvement plans, district improvement plan
September	School board strategic planning dates
October	School board negotiation schedule
November	Spring student testing schedules
December	Progress on school improvement plans
January	Results of student progress from first semester
February	Board initial budget plan for upcoming school year, board tax plan for upcoming year
March	District strategic plan for upcoming year
April	School configuration and staffing plans for the upcoming year
May	Progress on staff development plans
June	District and school improvement plan results, final school district budget balances, results of student achievement testing, results of board strategic planning

Superintendent to Board

One thing that separates good superintendents from great superintendents is constant communication with their board. Great superintendents constantly feed their board members information so they are rarely in the dark or surprised by the superintendent. It is important to provide the kind of information that supports the board in its roles of policymaking and budget management, while being careful not to open the door for micromanagement. Many superintendents spend a majority of their time working with the board to provide communication and support the roles in policy and budget management. Listed below are some of the common vehicles superintendents use in order to make this happen:

Board information flyers: Great superintendents spend time developing a weekly board information flyer that is delivered to board members. In these board information flyers the superintendent includes items such as announcements, inner-district memos, newspaper clippings, legislative updates, budget reports, reports on incidents happening in the school district and the administration's plans to deal with these incidents, progress on school improvement initiatives, and other documents that provide a window for board members to see how the district is operating and how the administration is working together to make decisions for the effective operation of the school district. Typically board information flyers contain both information that is open to the public and information that is confidential in nature. The superintendents utilizing these flyers clearly labels confidential information and remind board members not to share this information. Board information flyers are normally delivered toward the end of in operating week (typically Thursday afternoon) and are followed up with a phone call by the superintendent on Friday or during the weekend to make sure board members have received and read the information flyer and to see if they have any questions. Figure 9.8 is a template you can use to assist you in planning a board information flyer.

Regular phone communication: Great superintendents keep in touch with board members through regular phone communication. The person that gets the most regular contact is the board chair, followed closely by board officers. We have worked with superintendents who call the board chair every day and other board members at least twice each week. At first this amount of contact may seem too much and too time-consuming but in the end, small, percolating issues can be dealt with before they turn into great difficulties. As a result of regular phone communication, a superintendent can assess were board members are on particular issues, and can also decide his or her approach in working with the board to help them understand and act on issues appropriately. Having this regular phone contact with board members allows them to get to know the superintendent and trust his or her decision making capabilities. It also helps board members feel important and valued by the superintendent. This builds needed rapport for the relationship to work effectively. Use the phone log in Table 9.4 as a general guide to assist you in keeping track of your board phone communications.

Key Point #5: The superintendent–board communication process is foundational to your success and the success of the school district. Be sure you take the time to develop a solid and reliable communication process.

Internet and e-mail communication: Regular communication from superintendent to board can also be facilitated through effective e-mails. New superintendents need to be especially careful, though, when crafting written messages to ensure they clearly communicate the intent and

Figure 9.8 Board Information Flyer Planning Template

Board information need or desire:	Component to include in board information flyer to address need or desire:
What format would best serve the board in developing the board information flyer?	
What schedule should be used for delivery of the board information flyer? What kind of follow up will be implemented to ensure that board members understand the information provided to them in the flyer?	

Table 9.4   Board Member Phone Communication and Follow Up Log

Board Member Name	Date of Communication	Information Provided	Questions or Concerns Expressed by Board Member	Follow Up Needed

message intended. At times we are in a hurry and send a hastily developed e-mail that could come back to haunt us. We recommend that e-mail be used for simple, straightforward issues but should be augmented by personal follow up for concerns that are more complex and need further communication.

Board committees: Most boards typically divide themselves into working committees. The purpose of these committees can vary but they normally help the board understand certain aspects of school district decision making and possibly operation. Working committees also help to facilitate greater buy-in by other board members for decisions they need to act on. This is a prime time for a superintendent to communicate with individuals or small groups of board members. It is also an optimal to learn how these board members process information and make decisions. Superintendents should attend board committee meetings prepared to present the information and rationale that provides a foundation for decisions within their particular area of operation. A planning template is provided in Figure 9.9 to assist you in working with board committees to make the most of the experience.

Board to Community

Another area crucial to the success of a new superintendent is the level of communication that exists between the school board and the school district community. In most cases you are the one who is responsible for making sure that this communication happens. In the past, community members trusted their board and superintendents and did not have a high need for continuous communication about board issues and decisions and district operations. In today's world, our communities demand more information and seem to be less trusting of public boards and administrators. In order to help combat this situation as a new superintendent, you need to take a proactive stance on providing regular communication vehicles from the board to the community.

Community to Board

Some community members are interested in making their thoughts to the school board well known. Typically community members communicate directly with board members using the telephone, personal interactions at community events, e-mail, and public participation sessions at board meetings. Many times board members feel compelled to provide answers to members of the public when they're confronted or asked about district operations or decisions. As a new superintendent you can help your board work through these kinds of issues by providing them with a process they can use to avoid being put on the spot and having to come up with an instant answer to community members' concerns and questions.

Figure 9.9 Board Work Committee Planning Template

Use the following planning template to assist you as you begin to work with board work committees.

1. What are the general goals or tasks that this board committee is working to accomplish?

_____

_____

_____

2. What are you hoping that board members on this committee will learn about their work area, your skills as superintendent, and the skills of your staff members as a result of their participation?

_____

_____

_____

3. How do you plan to conduct the meeting so that your goals for board member learning are attained?

_____

_____

_____

4. How do you plan to assess the meeting to ensure that board members leave with the goals you have established at the committee meeting?

_____

_____

_____

5. What will you do if you notice that committee or staff members are not staying on task?

_____

_____

_____

Great superintendents work with their boards to adopt a board/community problem-solving protocol. Here is an example of a few steps superintendents have used over the years as a protocol for their boards:

- When confronted with a question from a community member, each board member can use one of two responses that will buy them the time to handle the situation appropriately:
  - "Please contact the superintendent about that issue."
  - "Let me talk about that issue with the superintendent and I will get back with you."

  These responses honor the individual's request for information, but also are aimed at allowing adequate time to provide accurate answers. In most situations community members will give you the time to follow this process, although if they press the issue board members can move to the next option, identified below.

- If the community member continues to press the board member, they can ask to speak with the individual privately and then record the concerns in writing. These concerns can then be brought back to the superintendent for further clarification.

If, for some reason, the community member is not willing to be reasonable, it may be that the board member will need to end the conversation. This is rare and would never be preferable, but may become necessary if the situation warrants such action.

As part of the board member/community communication process it is always important for school board members to indicate that their opinion represents them individually and not the thinking of the board as a corporate body. It is also important to communicate that only the board, as a corporate body, can make decisions or changes regarding district policy, goals, or direction.

Board to Superintendent

Communication between the board and superintendent should be frequent and aimed at achieving a team concept. The standards that are identified in the board operating protocol should also be followed in the board's communication with its superintendent. There are two primary issues we have seen over the years regarding board to superintendent communication. The first relates to "surprises." Some board members fail to communicate that an issue exists and then they choose to bring up the concern during a board meeting or at some other public meeting. Obviously this creates an embarrassing situation and must be discouraged. Alternatively, encourage board members to bring up new information in appropriate settings. During your annual board retreat be sure to review standards such as "no surprises" so that everyone is clear regarding how these situations should be handled.

Another concern that plagues board/superintendent communication is that some board members do not follow boundaries regarding requests of the superintendent and/or the district's staff. These oftentimes are your "micromanaging" board members who feel they don't need to make requests as a corporate body, but rather want their issues handled immediately and without transparency. A method some superintendents have used to address this issue is that when a request is made, they send the request to all other board members indicating they are doing the research and it will be available on a certain date. This keeps all board members informed of individual requests and minimizes micromanaging board members from operating "under the radar."

HANDLING PRIVATE AND PUBLIC DATA

Understanding the difference between private and public data is very important for superintendents. You will be engaged in many confidential matters and will receive requests for information from a variety of people. You need to understand what you can share and with whom.

The first step in this process is to learn the laws about data privacy and confidential information in your state. All districts nationwide are governed by the Federal Educational Records Privacy Act (FERPA), which provides guidance related to what can be shared regarding students and their records. In addition, most states provide further guidance that should be understood as well. In fact, these statutes in most cases also govern employee data. Often both state and federal regulations are outlined in your board policy. Be sure to review the policies that regulate the handling of private and public data so that you can be safe regarding your communications.

A helpful method to manage these regulations is to summarize the law and your policies on a card that can be referred to periodically to refresh your memory. Many superintendents keep this information in the top drawer of their desk for quick reference. You will be surprised how many times you pull out this information and refer to it prior to taking action.

Another helpful tip used by some superintendents is to establish a filing and coding system for public and private information. This enables you to be clear regarding what is public data and can be quickly shared upon request, and what is private data and must be handled with greater caution. You can ask your secretary to assist in establishing a system that can be used during your tenure in the district. In fact, it is appropriate to send your secretary through training so that he or she can manage these data for you prior to your review.

SUMMARY

One of the most significant measures of a superintendent's success rests in his or her ability to effectively communicate with various constituencies. Communication is not just the act of delivering information, but also managing it to meet the district's needs.

In this chapter we discussed key issues that are important to your success in the superintendency. Let's review a few things to remember regarding effective communication strategies:

- Be sure to identify your core values and communicate from these thoughts and ideas. To the extent that you can develop key messages regarding each facet of the school district's operation you will find it easier to address the public in various settings.
- Remember if you identify potential objections (possibly through the Sticky Notes Ripple Effect process) and address them when communicating your decisions, you minimize negative reaction to your message.
- Superintendents who use information flow charts find communications are clearer and more effective.
- Assisting your board regarding how it communicates with different constituencies can have a very positive impact on the district's operation. Often board members are not trained, nor have they pondered how to communicate with different constituencies.
- Understanding public and private information and what can and cannot be shared will save superintendents many headaches. Be sure to review the district's policies related to public and private information and develop an index card to follow in challenging times.

The first time most superintendents enter into large group communication is when the new school year begins. They need to address the staff, begin attending service club meetings, and hold other events as well. In Chapter 10, It's July, Now What?, we help you begin thinking about these first few months of the school year. This chapter is full of ideas to get you started, from establishing an entry plan to your first staff meeting to creating a monthly calendar of events.

10

It's July, Now What?

The leadership instinct you are born with is the back-bone. You develop the funny bone and the wishbone that go with it.

—Elaine Agather

Most superintendents start in July and experience a reprieve; they can get their office set up, establish an entry plan, and begin to meet key constituents in the school district. This is a nice time as it represents the lull before the storm and being the "new kid on the block," most every interaction is positive. You are enjoying many social events aimed at helping you meet those who have influence in the district and things are generally upbeat.

School will begin shortly and you need to prepare for everything from the first day to establishing yourself as the district's new leader with your staff. We have divided this chapter into four sections; each includes help-ful tools to get you started in your superintendency.

ABOUT THIS CHAPTER

This chapter outlines some of the more common issues and tasks that you will face as a new superintendent. It is set up slightly different than other chapters because the topics are not in any particular thematic structure, but rather are organized around the various months of the year and when needs arise. As you read the information in this chapter pay particular attention to the following information:

- Developing an entry plan to assist you in learning about your school district
- How to plan for the opening day with staff
- The importance of finding an experienced, knowledgeable mentor
- A list of activities to consider during your initial year in the district

THE IMPORTANCE OF AN ENTRY PLAN: SUCCESSFULLY NAVIGATING YOUR FIRST NINETY DAYS ON THE JOB

The superintendent position will likely be the most complicated job you will have during your professional career. Unlike most positions the superintendent is expected to be in touch with parents, staff, administration, board, students, community, business leaders, clergy, elected officials, and service organizations, and the list goes on and can vary depending upon the community.

How can you get up to speed and establish yourself as the district's new leader? The answer is through developing an entry plan. Entry plans can vary in length, scope, and end date, but need to focus on introducing you to the community and provide an overview of the school district operation.

To start, it is important to include individual meetings with school board members, community leaders, key administrators, and supervisors as part of your entry plan. During these meetings you can determine people's perceptions of the strengths and weaknesses of the school district and begin to understand their expectations for your first year. This is also a good time to talk about your plans for the district and "test the water" concerning key initiatives that you may be considering.

Vital to your success is a plan that enables you to become well established in your new position. If well designed you will get an "insider's" view of the community and school district organization. This, in turn, will prepare you politically as you move ahead with needed changes and new initiatives.

Figure 10.1 provides a sample entry plan that you can modify for use in your district. Although formats can vary, the goal is always the same: to acquaint yourself with the school district operation and identify key issues that must be immediately addressed. It is important to design your entry plan to address at least the first ninety days of your tenure. This is important as the first ninety days will be about getting to know the district, its people, and establishing a baseline understanding of its unique characteristics. Once you become familiar with the district, you can then begin the process of developing your goals. You will also find that clearly outlining how to approach your first ninety days on the job will establish a solid foundation for your success in the superintendency. The board, staff, and community will see that you have a plan and will appreciate your level of preparation. In addition we have provided a sample report in the appendix section, which shows how one superintendent presented her entry plan findings to the board of education.

> **Key Point #1:** Developing an entry plan as you begin your tenure will ensure you have established a comprehensive approach to becoming acquainted with the district.

Consider the following tips when designing your entry plan:

Figure 10.1   New Superintendent Sample Entry Plan

Achievement Valley Schools

Entry Plan for the Superintendent of Schools

Outcomes

- Establish a plan for approaching the first ninety days as superintendent
- Begin to develop key relationships with school district and community constituents
- Assess current school district issues and concerns
- Identify the formal and informal policies, procedures, and communication strategies within the district
- Identify issues to be addressed, establish a list of priorities, and develop an action plan

Activities

Constituency Group

Board

- Review the roles and responsibilities of the Board of Education and superintendent
- Clarify the superintendent–board chair relationship
- Develop a board operating protocol
- Establish an entry plan with input from the Board

(Continued)

Figure 10.1   (Continued)

District Office

- Determine organizational norms and structure of the district office
- Clarify the roles and relationship of each person in the office
- Analyze areas where coordination and alignment are required

Building Administrators

- Determine key issues and main concerns school leaders face in the coming year
- Determine how the work of the principals can best be supported
- Analyze site versus district office responsibilities
- Analyze the climate for learning and self-reflection

Employee Groups

- Understand the relationship between the associations and the district
- Define associations' issues and concerns
- Design communication format

Students

- Understand the issues which are important to students
- Establish communication with key student leaders and student groups

Teachers

- Understand the structure, membership, and responsibilities of teacher groups (collaboration groups, planning groups, grade level teams, departments, etc.)
- Listen to hopes, desires, and concerns
- Identify teachers' ideas for change
- Explore with teachers what they believe is going well

Parents

- Establish a relationship with school-related organizations
- Understand the contribution these organizations make to the school district
- Listen to parents' hopes and desires for their children's schools

Community

- Gather perceptions of the school district from within the community
- Determine "school district message" to be conveyed
- Create understanding and enhance community support for the schools

Data Collection Methods

- Identify and interview key personnel (listed below)
- Conduct focus groups with key community organizations and leaders, teachers, support staff, students, parents
- Visit district schools
- Analyze the data collected
- Provide feedback to the various groups within the organization

Interviews to be Scheduled

- Board members
- Building administrators
- Business manager
- Support staff (secretaries, food service, maintenance, transportation, etc.)
- Athletic director
- Association presidents
- Department chairs, teachers on special assignment, and other out of classroom personnel
- Student leaders
- PTA or PTO
- Parents
- Community
  1. City officials
  2. Police chief
  3. Fire chief
  4. State representatives
  5. Neighboring school superintendents
  6. Service organizations
  7. Senior citizens
  8. Clergy
  9. Other contacts as determined by the board and superintendent

(Continued)

Figure 10.1 (Continued)

Document Review	
• Strategic plan	• District promotional brochures
• Employee agreements and grievances	• Key state reports
• Budget documents	• Accreditation reports
• Policies	• Annual financial report/audit
• Administrative procedures	• Board agendas and minutes
• Administrator job descriptions	• Special education program evaluations/reviews
• Key personnel evaluations	• Grants
• Content standards, curriculum maps, and pacing guides	• Capital improvement plan
• School improvement plans	• Technology plan
• Student and faculty handbooks	• Crisis management plans

Studies to Conduct (Studies may take longer than ninety days)
- Curriculum audit
- Communications audit

SOURCE: Adapted from Westbrook Public Schools, Westbrook, CT.

- Don't underestimate the importance of developing relationships with the district's key communicators.
- Be sure to thoroughly understand both the formal and hidden leadership structures of the school district.
- Listen for what the culture of the district and community value in their schools.
- Take the first ninety days of your tenure, using the entry plan process, to consider potential goals for your efforts in the district.

Key Point #2: Develop an entry plan that will introduce you to the district, its operations, and unique context.

OPENING DAY WITH STAFF

As you enter the superintendency you are challenged by the specter of "opening day." You most likely will ask yourself: What do I say? What does the staff expect? How do I want to establish myself? These and many other questions will be pulsing through your mind as you prepare for that important first opportunity to address the staff.

Realize that although everyone is interested in hearing your initial remarks, they are also seeing each other for the first time after a summer's long hiatus. This is important because in any preparation you undertake for this first morning, you need to set aside an initial period of time (one hour) where people can talk and catch up on the summer's events. Doing so will enable them to feel much more relaxed and willing to hear what the "new" superintendent has to say.

Once they have been provided ample time for conversation and the program begins, make your part of the process both fun and informative. Your staff will enjoy hearing that you are excited to get to know them personally and that you enjoyed, as an example, the community's Fourth of July parade. A human connection always opens people's minds to your message. Then, once it is time to talk about your vision and plans for the district, keep the message simple and focused on a few memorable topics. Your goal is to have them leave with a few "sound bites" of information that will be the beginning of your tenure in the school district.

A sample agenda for your first day is provided in Figure 10.2. Opening day events are typically planned by a group, but the format outlined below gives you a sense of what this process might look like.

Figure 10.2　Sample Opening Day Agenda

Welcome Back Breakfast

Opening Day Celebration Location: Pioneer Middle School

Date & Time: Wednesday, August 22, 8:00–10:30 AM

Welcome Back Breakfast Agenda

8:00–8:45	Breakfast Served by Board of Education and Administrators
8:45–9:00	Welcome back messages: • Tom Jones, Superintendent • Leslie Smith, Board Chair • Cheryl Tiff, President, Teachers' Association
9:00–9:30	Employee Recognition Ceremony (Recognizing employees for their years of service) Tom Jones, Superintendent; Cheryl Tiff, Teachers' Association; Bill Edwards, United Custodial Association; Jennifer Wright, Association of Office Workers; Jill Banger, District 121 Bus Drivers' Association
9:30–10:30	Strategic Plan and Implementation Process for the Upcoming School Year Tom Jones, Superintendent
10:30–3:00	Building Level Meetings

Consider the following tips when planning opening day activities:

- Be sure to provide ample time for the staff to visit prior to starting the program.
- Establish a group to help plan the opening day celebration.
- Consider adding a bit of humor and personal connection to your opening day remarks. The staff will want to hear your vision for the district, but will also want to make a connection with you as an individual.
- Always remember to make food part of any opening day event.

Key Point #3: Be sure that as part of your opening day activities you make a personal connection with the audience. This helps people to see you as "human" and embrace your thoughts, ideas, and comments.

SELECTING A MENTOR

When new to a superintendency, a mentor can help you transition into the job seamlessly. One of the more crucial decisions you will make is in the selection of the person who will "show you the ropes." How do you identify and select an appropriate mentor? In speaking with seated superintendents and through our own observation and tenure in the superintendency we have developed a list of key components to consider in establishing a successful mentor–mentee relationship.

Key Components for Successful Mentor–Mentee Relationships

- Look for someone you can trust.
- Assess your potential mentor for job performance credibility.
- Look for a match in the district size, complexity, and needs.
- Examine the potential mentor's ability to listen, coach, and communicate.
- Look for a personality match.
- Make sure your potential mentor has gone through a situation similar to what you face.
- Assess the person's ability to keep your conversations confidential.
- Understand your potential mentor's ability to break down complex tasks and explain them clearly.

To assist you in further understanding the importance of these key components, we have expanded on them below. The mentor–mentee relationship, if properly designed, has the power to take your initial experience in the superintendency from one of isolation and reactive action to one of collegial support and reflective decision making.

Look for someone you can trust: Above all, trusting your mentor is the most crucial aspect of the relationship. You should be able to place confidence in the ideas and suggestions they provide you. You should have a good feeling about talking with this person. The advice you get should resonate well with you. How do you assess for trust? Most of us have a good sense when it comes to other people. As you initially interact with your colleagues, look for a potential mentor who has established positive connections and relationships with others. This type of person may seek you out and offer congratulations on your new assignment. You should feel good about your conversations and the connections you have established with this person. He or she will be a close colleague of yours and provide much support throughout your initial transition. Trust your intuition and choose wisely.

Assess your potential mentor for job performance credibility: Your mentor's ability to perform in the superintendency is another important aspect of the mentor relationship you need to take into consideration. The reasons here are obvious, but unless he or she is competent, a mentor can't give you good advice. This person does not have to be the former "superintendent of the year" to help you, but should be competent in the core skills of the position. You can assess this person's competency by listening to your colleagues, asking your administrative staff for their perceptions, and seeing how this person interacts with others in your collegial group.

Look for a match in the district size, complexity, and needs: If your mentor is to give you sound advice, it is important that this person understands the context in which you will be working. This can best be achieved if he or she has some experience in a situation that is somewhat aligned with what you presently face. As you consider different potential mentors, look at the district they lead to see if there are similarities. Factors you may wish to assess include size, student demographics, physical plant conditions, board make-up, geographic location, and any other issues you deem important. If the potential mentor candidate does not work in a situation (or has not worked in a situation) that directly matches yours, it will be hard for this person to provide information and ideas that can help you succeed.

Examine the potential mentor's ability to listen, coach, and communicate: The most effective mentors spend more time listening to you than in giving you advice. When we are first involved in a mentoring relationship we sometimes seek out the opinions and ideas of others. In the long run, however, you will be the person who ultimately needs to decide how to move forward on an issue. Good mentors will help you develop a frame of reference to take in information, weigh all the options, and make a final decision on an issue. As you engage in conversations with your mentor, be sure to pay attention to the ratio of how many times you are told what to do rather than assisted in making your own decisions. Choose someone who will listen and help you to grow.

Look for a personality match: It is obvious that your mentor's personality needs to enhance your own effectiveness. Sometimes it is important for us to select a mentor who sees things differently from us and helps us to expand our field of vision. At other times, we need to work with people who match our personalities and resonate with our thoughts. As a new superintendent, assess your needs and select a mentor who will connect with you while helping you grow as a professional.

Make sure your potential mentor has gone through a situation similar to what you face: This aspect is closely related to an area that was presented earlier in this section. Examine the major issues you anticipate facing during your first year as a superintendent and seek out an individual who has faced a similar situation. If your employee contracts have not yet been settled, you may want to consider a mentor who has had to deal with contentious employee negotiations. If your board needs support to become effective as a decision making body seek out someone who has faced a similar state. The experience that a mentor brings to the table can help you achieve success as you address tough issues during your first year on the job.

Assess the person's ability to keep your conversations confidential: You will be exposing yourself, your weaknesses, and possibly confidential situations to your mentor. Make sure this person has the integrity to respect your confidentiality in every situation you choose to share. Work into the relationship gradually, observe how your mentor interacts with others, observe whether your mentor talks in a negative manner about people not present in meetings on a regular basis, and see if this person "volunteers" to share secrets about other colleagues. All of these behaviors are indicators that there is a lack of integrity. Use your intuition in making a decision about further engaging this potential mentor in a deeper relationship.

Understand your potential mentor's ability to break down complex tasks and explain them clearly: A mentor helps you understand situations and figure out how to move forward on issues. This kind if assistance requires that a person is able to look at the component parts of a "whole" situation. Look for a mentor who is able to break a complex task down into parts. Find a mentor who understands there is an order and a hierarchy to making complex decisions. When your mentor can see the big picture, and at the same time look at the parts, the guidance this person provides will be crucial to your success.

If you consider all of the categories that were discussed in this section, you should be able to select a mentor who can truly help you become a successful superintendent. At times, no one person may possess all of the skills needed to be an effective mentor. Many new superintendents seek several people to help them make a smooth transition into the job. One colleague may help you with budget questions, while another can provide guidance in building superintendent–board relations. In many cases, a new superintendent will select someone to be their primary mentor while seeking situational guidance from a small circle of additional colleagues. Be sure you take the time to consider your needs and find a mentor who has the ability to draw out your strengths.

It is also important to realize that although your state association, or some other organization, may "assign" a mentor to you as part of a pre-designed program, you need to be mindful of the components we have outlined above. The person assigned to you may fit all the key components we discussed earlier, although they may become only one of the individuals you will use in your mentor–mentee relationship(s). Remember that only you can seek out individuals who will be helpful to you in establishing this relationship. Protect your ability to remain flexible in finding mentors who meet the criteria described earlier.

Consider the following tips when selecting a mentor:

- Find an individual who has a broad knowledge base and can help you in a variety of situations.
- Be sure you can trust your mentor to keep sensitive information confidential.
- Engage someone who has a "true interest" in serving as a mentor.
- Look for someone who can serve as a coach and who has the ability to look at issues analytically.

Key Point #4: Be sure to select a mentor who you respect and who is truly interested in serving in this role.

SAMPLE CALENDAR OF MONTHLY EVENTS/ACTIVITIES

Below we have provided a monthly calendar of events and activities you are likely to face in the superintendency. It is important to use this list as a guide, but to develop your own calendar for the year. Following this process will enable you to approach your initial year with confidence knowing the issues to be faced. Once you have this knowledge you can then begin to effectively plan for upcoming events.

July

- Plan "Welcome Back/Opening Day" district event.
- Prepare for opening staff workshops/staff development.
- Review/revise crisis management plan.
- Publish annual legal notices.
- Conduct retreat to develop board and administrative team goals for upcoming year.
- Build superintendent finance reference binder.
- Prepare new school year newsletter for parents.
- Plan teacher mentorship program activities for the year.
- Review district's marketing plan for the upcoming year.
- Facilitate school board evaluation.

August

- Conduct summer staff/new teacher luncheon.
- Conduct "Welcome Back/Opening Day" activities for various employee groups.
- Conduct opening staff workshops/staff development.
- Start teacher mentorship activities.
- Plan monthly board meeting program review/recognition program (i.e., special education program, gifted and talented program, etc.).
- Review/discuss legislative statute changes with the board and administration.
- Conduct school board tour of summer construction/maintenance projects.
- Host a workshop for school board election candidates.
- Develop schedule and identify topics for internal and external district communications program.
- Ask business office to prepare monthly superintendent finance reports: revenue, expenditures, enrollment, and staffing plan/ Position Control System changes.
- Finalize staffing plan/Position Control System process.
- Develop schedule for school visitations.

September

- Review student enrollment (seat count) versus budgeted enrollment.
- Review evaluation schedule and responsibilities with supervisors.

- Review district-level and building improvement plans for the year.
- Deliver summer school report to the board.
- Update inclement weather procedure and call lists.
- Develop calendar of state and federal report due dates for administrative team.
- Prepare a written "Welcome Back" communication to parents.

October

- Ask for a review of previous year's audit with the district's auditor.
- Update long-range financial projections based upon the completed audit.
- Celebrate National School Lunch Week.
- Recognize National School Bus Safety Week.
- Complete benchmarking/dashboard report with data from comparison districts; test scores, levy amount(s), expenditures per pupil, demographic information, staff FTE, student FTE, etc.
- Prepare a written communication to the community which highlights school safety considerations for the new school year.

November

- Revise current year's budget.
- Draft budget development assumptions for upcoming year.
- Celebrate American Education Week.
- Celebrate National Community Education Day.
- Revise budget handbook for upcoming year.
- Conduct employee service award ceremony during American Education Week.
- Prepare a written communication to the community which celebrates the district's educators.

December

- Plan and conduct district holiday celebration(s).
- Set up January meeting with legislators.
- Visit building holiday celebrations.
- Develop upcoming year's school calendar.
- Prepare a written mid-year report for district residents.

January

- Conduct mid-year review of goals and performance pay measures.
- Distribute budget handbook and building allocations.

- Approve curricular changes for upcoming year.
- Begin review of personnel requests for upcoming year.
- Review and update long-range capital projects plan (to include technology).
- Prepare written news article on new educational programs which were introduced for the current school year.

February

- Compile retiree list for budget purposes and end of year recognition.
- Revise district facility use and activity fee levels for upcoming year.
- Revise/finalize enrollment projections for upcoming year.
- Prepare legislative priorities report for district residents.

March

- Begin conducting annual employee evaluations.
- Plan summer school program.
- Finalize upcoming year's draft staffing /Position Control System plan.
- Draft school district marketing plan for upcoming year.
- Prepare written news article on the school district's upcoming spring activities.

April

- Develop district professional learning plan for upcoming year.
- Conduct volunteer recognition ceremony.
- Complete summer maintenance/remodeling plans.
- Review hiring procedures and priorities with principals.
- Prepare written news article of the district's student successes for the school year.

May

- Draft "state of the schools" report for distribution to the community.
- Identify school service award recipients for end of year recognition.
- Finalize employee layoff plan (as needed).
- Conduct kindergarten orientation.
- Conduct 360° review of superintendent's performance with staff and community.
- Review mentor/new teacher and administrator program for upcoming year.

June

- Adopt upcoming year's budget.
- Hire consultant to provide guidance with levy/bond (as needed).
- Conduct phone poll for levy/bond early in the month (as needed).
- Conduct retirement recognition ceremony.
- Review long-range financial plan with board.
- Conduct year-end interview with board regarding perceptions of accomplishments, district needs, and potential goals.
- Finalize sub teacher salary, lunch price, and other fee recommendations for the upcoming year.
- Finalize board and administration retreat plans.
- Facilitate superintendent's evaluation with the board.

Consider the following tips when building your calendar of monthly activities/events:

- Be sure to track your actual activities each month of the year so that your calendar is based in reality in year two.
- Prepare a written communication to the community each month of the school year.
- Ask others what should be included in your calendar during the entry plan process.

Key Point #5: Developing a monthly calendar of events and tasks which must be remembered will help you stay organized during your initial year in the superintendency.

SUMMARY

The initial year of your superintendency will move by quickly, with events coming at you faster than you might be able to plan and react. This chapter was designed as a "catch all" to help you as you work through that important first year. The strategies and ideas listed have been tried and tested by others who have successfully navigated the superintendency.

As you think about what you have learned as a result of this chapter consider the following questions:

- What is the importance of an entry plan? What key components need to be in place for the plan to be successful?

- What characteristics should you consider when selecting a mentor? How will you assess these components in individuals you are considering as a possible mentor?
- What important events need to happen during the first ninety days of your superintendency? What do you need to do in order to effectively plan for the smooth implementation of these events?
- What have you learned as a result of reading this chapter? How will you put your learning into operation?

As you can see, there is much work to do as a new superintendent in order to be successful. Obviously, you have the skills and potential to do a good job; all you have to do is implement, right?

In this book we have tried to provide you with a basic foundation in order to begin the process of building a successful superintendency. Like most situations in life, you will be the person responsible for your own success as you move forward in the position. We understand circumstances will present themselves that are out of your direct control. In some cases people allow circumstances to control them; you will need to find ways to work within the structure of your role and the situations you will face to achieve success in the superintendency. We hope the ideas and strategies presented in this book will help you as you enter this rewarding and challenging stage of your career.

Good luck, and we wish you a long and successful tenure as a superintendent.

Key Points
From Each Chapter

Chapter 1

Key Point #1: Understand your importance and visibility as the superintendent; be sure to use these components of the position to achieve the district's goals.

Key Point #2: As the superintendent you are expected to be able to see things from the "big picture" or in relation to the best interests of the community.

Key Point #3: Be careful during your initial meetings with employees/constituents so that you don't get trapped, engage in negative conversations, or make unreasonable promises with those who may be "jockeying for position."

Key Point #4: It's important for you to be able to "see" the view or perspective of others before you move forward on an idea or plan. Once you have identified their views, you can begin to work to help them see the wider perspective in relation to the idea or plan.

Key Point #5: Understand your role in serving as a community liaison. In this role you will serve as a sort of conduit between the community and the school district.

Key Point #6: Understand the attributes of effective change before attempting to move new initiatives or plans forward. This is an idea that will help you transcend a changing school landscape.

Key Point #7: Identify the principles that provide the foundation for your ideas and opinions. Be able to clearly and concisely share them related to the major decisions you will face. Don't "dig in" on issues over stubbornness, but do take a stand when an issue is directly related to one of your core foundational values.

Key Point #8: As you begin your superintendency, keep effective communication strategies at the forefront of your most important behaviors. Be sure to think about effective two-way communication and the integration of spoken, written, and nonverbal methods in your tool kit.

Chapter 2

Key Point #1: Be aware of the fact that how you interact with individual board members and respond to their requests will set the stage for how you are perceived. Take care to establish patterns of equal treatment with your board.

Key Point # 2: Consider the unique needs of individual board members when working to provide them with "equal treatment and information."

Key Point #3: Do not leave role expectations with your board chair/president to chance. Assist the board in identifying/clarifying this important role and your responsibilities in the working relationship.

Key Point #4: Keep in mind that the individual you will speak with most in the district is the board chair/president. Understand the complexity of this unique relationship and take the necessary steps to ensure success.

Key Point #5: The most important relationship you will need to nurture is the one between you and your board; you will need to put together a purposeful communication plan to build this relationship.

Key Point #6: In the establishment of your communication plan, be sure to address communication forms and frequency.

Key Point #7: Be purposeful in designing a process related to when and how you will make contact with your board when emergency situations arise.

Key Point #8: Periodically review the impact of your communication plan with your board members. Make the necessary adjustments and refinements to your plan and your strategies to maintain good superintendent–board relations.

Chapter 3

Key Point #1: Take time to get to know the culture of your district. Culture can be difficult to change quickly, so be sure you have a thorough understanding of its nuances prior to moving forward.

Key Point #2: Remember that trust is an important commodity for you to possess as a superintendent. The amount a trust you have may depend on your ability to connect and build confidence with others.

Key Point #3: Since many people will be judging you based on their expectations rather than reality, try to open up communications about their expectations whenever possible. This behavior will go a long way in helping you meet expectations and build trust within your school community.

Key Point #4: In order to build a trusting atmosphere you will need to conduct some activities that let people get to know you and allow you to understand their expectations for you in your role as their superintendent.

Key Point #5: Keep in mind that your school district is made up of people and that people can be unpredictable and emotional. Don't underestimate the power of emotions in an organization. Responding appropriately can help enhance your sense of trust in the district.

Key Point #6: The union/association relationship is important for you as the superintendent. Pay close attention to these relationships so you don't have any major employee group working behind your back to undermine you in your new role.

Chapter 4

Key Point #1: Don't just rely on the expertise of your business manager to keep you informed about the district's financial status; find ways to quickly learn how to assess the financial health of the school district.

Key Point #2: Work with your district's finance and/or enrollment staff to generate enrollment reports that clearly tie to school funding based on how your particular state determines this funding. If you don't, you may be basing your budget assumptions on "head count" rather than figures that translate to your school district's income. A disaster could result from this miscalculation.

Key Point #3: Keep an eye on enrollment trends in the current school year and tie them back to the historical trends that your district has gathered. This correlation will help you as you work with your board and staff in making decisions related to the budget.

Key Point #4: Be conservative in your hiring practices, especially in situations where it appears the school district is experiencing rapid growth. The growth could disappear and your budget could be negatively impacted by the fact that you now have people on staff that you must pay for out of reserves or even borrowed money because the enrollment is not supporting their positions.

Key Point #5: Consider periodically performing a professionally conducted demographic study to give you reliable and accurate data upon which to make enrollment projections.

Key Point #6: If you are considering implementing a "Cohort Survival Study," be sure you consult state school finance organizations or school finance texts for proper procedures and implementation strategies. These sources can help raise the reliability of your study.

Key Point #7: Insist that your district's financial reports contain a description of the current year's budget, the current month's expenditures, the previous year's expenditures correlated to the particular month, and the percentage of the amount of the budget remaining expressed both in dollars and as a percentage.

Key Point #8: Be sure to include the amount of money left in the current budget on your budget reports. This figure should be expressed as a percentage but also may be expressed as a dollar amount. Some superintendents also include a comparison of the amount left in the current budget as it compares to last year's budget.

Key Point #9: Consider tracking revenues in your budgeting process. Even though in some states revenues come at different times and on a sporadic timeline, your understanding of the exact revenues will help you in your decision making role with the board and the community.

Key Point #10: Use long-range planning to provide clarity and predictability in the budgeting process.

Key Point #11: Spend some time with officials from the firm conducting your audit (the audit manager or partner is best) to ask the question: "What should I understand about this year's audit?"

Chapter 5

Key Point #1: Take time to understand the change process and the idea of building meaning for the vision before moving into a major change as the superintendent.

Key Point #2: Take time to build relationships and an understanding of the school district's needs and assets before launching a major initiative by yourself. Make sure you have engaged the support of key groups and individuals before moving forward.

Key Point #3: Develop a plan to utilize your "honeymoon" period to gain a better understanding of your district and maximize your change agenda.

Chapter 6:

Key Point #1: Keep the needs of your senior-level cabinet members and principals in mind when you are considering your supervision strategies.

Key Point #2: An emotionally safe workplace does not preclude you from talking about difficult issues. It does require that you put in place stable policies and practices for your employees.

Key Point #3: Even though you may be tempted to "get involved" in the operation of the various departments and schools under your indirect supervision, be sure to work through your directors and principals to keep them "in charge." In the long-term this will ensure a smoother operation and let you focus on more global, systemwide issues.

Key Point #4: When supervising employees, keep their need for feedback in mind. Be sure to provide both positive and refinement feedback to help them continue to grow in their roles.

Key Point #5: Use a variety of data sources when gathering information to evaluate the performance of divisions or departments. This will help you make sure that you get a balanced look at these divisions or departments and provide guidance to help improve their operation.

Key Point #6: Goal setting can be a highly effective and motivating way to implement director evaluation. Keep in mind that before anyone is allowed to participate in goal setting, that person should be meeting district standards for his or her job area.

Chapter 7

Key Point #1: Your role as an instructional leader should be prominent as the superintendent. Be sure to think about the ways you could model and provide influence on the instructional mission of the school district.

Key Point #2: The selection and recruitment of instructional staff can be one of the most important decisions you can make as the school district's instructional leader. Make sure you have a role in this process in your district.

Key Point #3: Your support and supervision of principals can have a positive impact on the level of student success and achievement in your district. Keep student learning at the forefront of your conversations and discussions related to principals and building operations.

Key Point #4: The phrase "putting your money where your mouth is" applies to your budgeting practices as they relate to student learning. Get in the habit of asking yourself, "How does this area we are considering spending money on impact student learning?" every time you consider a budgetary item. This practice will help you maintain your focus on students and their learning.

Chapter 8

Key Point #1: As a superintendent you deal with people who come from a variety of backgrounds and experiences. Many of them may bring issues from other experiences to their interations with you. Try to consider the origins of negative behavior as you work with others.

Key Point #2: At times, people who have strong beliefs or negative feelings may have trouble easily letting them go. Don't try to make people let go of strong feelings too quickly. Give them time and space to begin to soften their position on issues.

Key Point #3: Take some time to think about the background experiences of the people you are working with. You may get some ideas related to how they attained their perceptions and ideas.

Key Point #4: Understanding the specific type of conflict can help you decide how to support those people in your district.

Key Point #5: Temporarily withholding your opinion can allow people the time needed to think about and work through their issues. It also gives you time to think about your own response to a situation.

Key Point #6: Effective framing statements help to constrain conversations and put you in control. Reflecting statements help the other party to hear that you understand their perspective. Both of these elements help to set and maintain a collaborative relationship.

Key Point #7: When choosing to mediate, be sure to carefully assess the situation to see if you will be able to effectively deal with the situation and still come out as an interested third party. At times people who have tried to mediate have lost in the exchange because rather than fix the situation they just made both parties mad.

Chapter 9

Key Point #1: Identifying your core values is essential to effective communication. It allows you to think and focus.

Key Point #2: Focusing your key messages allows you to be prepared when you are asked to clarify or justify your position on issues in either public or private settings.

Key Point #3: Being ready to deal with objections allows you to seamlessly answer concerns without looking defensive.

Key Point #4: Information flow charts can be very helpful when you are facing situations that involve emotional information. They allow you to move forward in notifying key constituents and members of your community even in difficult times.

Key Point #5: The superintendent–board communication process is foundational to your success and the success of the school district. Be sure you take the time to develop a solid and reliable communication process.

Chapter 10

Key Point #1: Developing an entry plan as you begin your tenure will ensure you have established a comprehensive approach to becoming acquainted with the district.

Key Point #2: Develop an entry plan that will introduce you to the district, its operations, and unique context.

Key Point #3: Be sure that as part of your opening day activities you make a personal connection with the audience. This helps people to see you as "human" and embrace your thoughts, ideas, and comments.

Key Point #4: Be sure to select a mentor who you respect and who is truly interested in serving in this role.

Key Point #5: Developing a monthly calendar of events and tasks which must be remembered will help you stay organized during your initial year in the superintendency.

References

Abbott, M., & Clark, M. E. (2004). *Fiscal fitness: A guide to monitoring your school district's budget*. Albany, NY: New York State School Boards Association.

Bolman, L., & Deal, T. (1997). *Reframing organizations: Artistry, choice, and leadership*. San Francisco: Jossey-Bass.

Bork, L. (1993, May). Effective schools—effective superintendents: The emerging instructional leadership role. *Journal of School Leadership, 3*.

Bridges, W. (1991). *Managing transitions: Making the most of change*. Reading, MA: Perseus Books.

Chapman, C. (1997). *Becoming a superintendent: Challenges of school district leadership*. Upper Saddle River, NJ: Merrill Prentice Hall.

Covey, S., (1989). *The seven habits of highly effective people*. New York: Free Press.

Eller, J., & Eller, S. (2006). *Energizing staff meetings*. Thousand Oaks, CA: Corwin Press.

Eller, J. (2004). *Effective group facilitation in education: How to energize meetings and manage difficult groups*. Thousand Oaks, CA: Corwin Press.

Folger, J., Poole, M., & Stutman, R. (1993). *Working through conflict: Strategies for relationships, groups, and organizations*. White Plains, NY: Longman.

Fullan, M. (2001). *Leading in a culture of change*. San Francisco: Jossey-Bass.

Gardner, H. (2004). *Changing minds: The art and science of changing our own and other people's minds*. Boston, MA: Harvard Business School Press.

Glass, T., Björk, L., & Brunner, C. C. (2000). *The study of the American Superintendency 2000: A look at the superintendent in the new millennium*. Reston, VA: American Association of School Superintendents.

Goleman, D. (2004). *Primal leadership*. Boston, MA: Harvard Business School Press.

Guskey, T. (2000). *Evaluating professional development*. Thousand Oaks, CA: Corwin Press.

Hanson, M. E (1998). *Educational administration and organizational behavior*. Needham Heights, MA: Simon & Schuster Company.

Kochanek, J. (2005). *Building trust for better schools*. Thousand Oaks, CA: Corwin Press.

Kotter, J. (1996). *Leading change: Emotional aspects of the change process*. Boston, MA: Harvard Business School Press.

Kouzes, J., & Posner, B. (2007). *The leadership challenge*. San Francisco, CA: Jossey-Bass.

Kuhn, T. (1962). *The structure of scientific revolutions*. Chicago: University of Chicago Press.

March, J. G., & Olsen, J. P. (1979). *Ambiguity and choice in organizations,* 2nd edition, Bergen: Universitetsforlaget.

Moore-Johnson, S. (1996). *Leading to change: The challenge of the new superintendency.* San Francisco: Jossey-Bass.

Pritchett, P. (2002). *Shaping corporate culture.* Dallas, TX: Pritchett Publishing Company.

Schein, E. (1997). *Organizational culture and leadership.* San Francisco, CA: Jossey-Bass.

Senge, P. (1989). *The fifth discipline.* New York: Doubleday.

Wheatley, M. (1995). *Leadership and the new science.* New York: Barret Kohler Publishers.

Several quotes at the beginning of chapters were taken from the Web site http://www.quoteland.com.

Erma Bombeck, "If Life Is a Bowl of Cherries..." 1971
http://www.quoteland.com/topic.asp?CATEGORY_ID=302

Joyce Brothers
http://www.quoteland.com/topic.asp?CATEGORY_ID=462

Oscar Wilde
http://www.quoteland.com/author.asp?AUTHOR_ID=67

Mary Kay Ash
http://www.quoteland.com/topic.asp?CATEGORY_ID=137

Max De Pree, "Leadership Is an Art"
http://www.quoteland.com/topic.asp?CATEGORY_ID=91

Forest Witcraft
http://www.quoteland.com/topic.asp?CATEGORY_ID=267

Sydney J. Harris
http://www.quoteland.com/topic.asp?CATEGORY_ID=46

Sylvia Ashton-Warner
http://www.quoteland.com/topic.asp?CATEGORY_ID=302

Elaine Agather
http://www.quoteland.com/topic.asp?CATEGORY_ID=91

Index

CORWIN PRESS

The Corwin Press logo—a raven striding across an open book—represents the union of courage and learning. Corwin Press is committed to improving education for all learners by publishing books and other professional development resources for those serving the field of PreK–12 education. By providing practical, hands-on materials, Corwin Press continues to carry out the promise of its motto: **"Helping Educators Do Their Work Better."**

AMERICAN ASSOCIATION OF SCHOOL ADMINISTRATORS

The American Association of School Administrators, founded in 1865, is the professional organization for more than 13,000 educational leaders across the United States. AASA's mission is to support and develop effective school system leaders who are dedicated to the highest quality public education for all children. For more information, visit www.aasa.org.